National Security Case Management: An Annotated Guide

Robert Timothy Reagan

Federal Judicial Center
2011

This Federal Judicial Center publication was undertaken in furtherance of the Center's statutory mission to develop and conduct research and education programs for the judicial branch. The views expressed are those of the author and not necessarily those of the Federal Judicial Center.

Contents

Table of Cases v

Introduction 1

Part I
Classified Information 3

    The Classified Information Procedures Act 3
    Classified Information Security Officers 6
    Security Clearances for Court Staff 7
    Security Clearances for Attorneys 9
    Handling and Storing Classified Information 12
    Sharing Classified Information with Criminal Defendants 17
    Discovery 18
    FISA Evidence 19
    Civil Cases 21
    Other Government Secrets 22
    Filings and Proceedings 23
    State-Secrets Privilege 27
    Silent Witness Rule 28
    Special Judicial Resources 28
    Courts of Appeals 29
    Putting the Cat Back in the Bag 32

Part II
Other Issues 33

    Attorney–Client Issues 33
        Criminal Justice Act Appointments 33
        Conflicts of Interest 34
        Communication 35
        Rapport 36
    Conditions of Detention 37
        Security 37
        Access to Counsel 38
        Mental Health 38
    Cultural Accommodation 39
    High Profile 40
        Gag Orders 40
        Media Attention 41
        Reserved Seating 42
        Remote Viewing 42
        Courtroom Displays of Support or Opposition 43
        Making Filings and Evidence Available to News Media 43
    Courthouse Security 44

Jury Issues	45
Size of Venire	45
Anonymous Jury	46
Jury Questionnaire	47
Sequestration	49
News of National Security Events	50
Special Evidence Issues	51
Witness Security	51
Foreign Evidence	53
Examination of High-Security Detainees	55
Senior Government Officers	55
Pro Se Issues	56

Table of Cases

First World Trade Center Bombing
    First World Trade Center Bombing
        United States v. Salameh (S.D.N.Y. 1:93-cr-180) 40, 46, 46, 48, 49, 57
    Plot to Bomb New York City Tunnels and Landmarks
        United States v. Abdel Rahman (S.D.N.Y. 1:93-cr-181) 13, 33, 34, 46, 48, 49, 50
    Plot to Bomb U.S. Airplanes in Southeast Asia
        United States v. Yousef (S.D.N.Y. 1:93-cr-180-4) 44, 57

Burma
    Horn v. Huddle (D.D.C. 1:94-cv-1756) 21, 24, 27

Kenya and Tanzania
    First Prosecution for 1998 Embassy Bombings
        United States v. El-Hage (S.D.N.Y. 1:98-cr-1023)
        .... 8, 10, 17, 18, 24, 34, 35, 36, 37, 38, 40, 43, 44, 46, 47, 48, 50, 51, 56
    Prosecution of a Guantánamo Bay Detainee for 1998 Embassy Bombings
        United States v. Ghailani (S.D.N.Y. 1:98-cr-1023-9) 18, 24, 33, 39, 42, 47, 48, 49, 51

Millennium Bomber
    United States v. Ressam (W.D. Wash. 2:99-cr-666) and
    United States v. Haouari (S.D.N.Y. 1:00-cr-15).................... 8, 14, 19, 35, 45, 46, 47, 50, 52, 54

Would-Be Spy
    United States v. Regan (E.D. Va. 1:01-cr-405) 10, 14

Detroit
    United States v. Koubriti (E.D. Mich. 2:01-cr-80778) 8, 10, 14, 41, 46, 47, 49, 49, 56

Twentieth Hijacker
    United States v. Moussaoui (E.D. Va. 1:01-cr-455)
    .... 10, 17, 24, 30, 32, 36, 40, 43, 45, 46, 47, 49, 57

American Taliban
    United States v. Lindh (E.D. Va. 1:02-cr-37) 14, 19, 22, 52, 55

September 11 Damages
    In re Terrorist Attacks on September 11, 2001 (S.D.N.Y. 1:03-md-1570),
    In re September 11 Litigation (S.D.N.Y. 1:21-mc-97), and
    Related Actions 14, 22, 28, 52

Guantánamo Bay
    In re Guantanamo Bay Detainee Litigation (D.D.C. 1:08-mc-442) and
    Related Actions 11, 14, 17, 21, 22, 25, 29, 35, 39, 54, 56

Dirty Bomber
    Padilla v. Rumsfeld (S.D.N.Y. 1:02-cv-4445),
    Padilla v. Hanft (D.S.C. 2:04-cv-2221),
    Padilla v. Rumsfeld (D.S.C. 2:07-cv-410),
    United States v. Hassoun (S.D. Fla. 0:04-cr-60001), and
    Related Actions 8, 11, 14, 17, 19, 25, 30, 35, 38, 39, 45, 46, 47, 49, 49, 52

Lackawanna
    United States v. Goba (W.D.N.Y. 1:02-cr-214) 33, 40, 42, 45

A Plot to Kill President Bush
    United States v. Abu Ali (E.D. Va. 1:05-cr-53) 11, 14, 17, 30, 52, 54

Paintball
United States v. Royer (E.D. Va. 1:03-cr-296),
United States v. Al-Timimi (E.D. Va. 1:04-cr-385),
United States v. Chandia (E.D. Va. 1:05-cr-401), and
United States v. Benkahla (E.D. Va. 1:06-cr-9) 5, 11, 19, 25, 36, 40

Minneapolis
United States v. Warsame (D. Minn. 0:04-cr-29) 5, 9, 11, 15, 20, 37, 38, 39

Mistaken Rendition
El-Masri v. Tenet (E.D. Va. 1:05-cv-1417) 15, 21, 27, 31

Detainee Documents
ACLU v. Department of Defense (S.D.N.Y. 1:04-cv-4151) 9, 21, 25

Prosecution of a Charity
United States v. Holy Land Foundation (N.D. Tex. 3:04-cr-240)
.... 9, 11, 15, 17, 20, 34, 49, 50, 52, 55

Chicago
United States v. Abu Marzook (N.D. Ill. 1:03-cr-978).................... 5, 9, 11, 15, 25, 37, 47, 53, 55

Giving State Secrets to Lobbyists
United States v. Franklin (E.D. Va. 1:05-cr-225) 5, 9, 11, 15, 23, 26, 28, 31, 56

Lodi
United States v. Hayat (E.D. Cal. 2:05-cr-240) 6, 9, 11, 19, 26

Warrantless Wiretaps
Hepting v. AT&T (N.D. Cal. 3:06-cv-672),
In re NSA Telecommunication Records Litigation (N.D. Cal. 3:06-md-1791),
Al-Haramain Islamic Foundation v. Bush (D. Or. 3:06-cv-274),
ACLU v. NSA (E.D. Mich. 2:06-cv-10204),
Terkel v. AT&T (N.D. Ill. 1:06-cv-2837),
Center for Constitutional Rights v. Bush (S.D.N.Y. 1:06-cv-313),
Electronic Privacy Information Center v. Department of Justice (D.D.C. 1:06-cv-96),
Electronic Frontier Foundation v. Department of Justice (D.D.C. 1:07-cv-403), and
Related Actions 9, 12, 15, 21, 26, 27, 29, 31, 32

Toledo
United States v. Amawi (N.D. Ohio 3:06-cr-719) and
Related Actions 20, 36, 37, 38, 45, 47, 48, 50, 53

Atlanta
United States v. Ahmed (N.D. Ga. 1:06-cr-147) ... 6, 9, 12, 16, 20, 27, 35, 40, 42, 42, 44, 48, 58

Sears Tower
United States v. Batiste (S.D. Fla. 1:06-cr-20373) 16, 47, 48, 50

Fort Dix
United States v. Shnewer (D.N.J. 1:07-cr-459)
.... 9, 12, 16, 17, 20, 27, 33, 42, 43, 44, 45, 47, 48, 50

Torture Flights
Mohamed v. Jeppesen DataPlan, Inc. (N.D. Cal. 5:07-cv-2798) 16, 22, 28, 31

Introduction

National security cases come in many types, including terrorism prosecutions, espionage prosecutions, and actions against the government concerning programs cloaked in secrecy.

A significant challenge faced by courts presiding over national security cases is the handling of classified information. Court proceedings and records are presumptively public, but courts are familiar with sealing selected proceedings and records to protect important secrets. Classified information, however, is a special type of secret, and its protection is controlled by the executive branch. Generally speaking, access to classified information requires a security clearance granted by the executive branch and a determination by the executive branch that the person granted access has a "need to know." Article III judges have automatic security clearances.

Other challenges that arise in national security cases, especially criminal prosecutions, are often very similar to issues that arise in other cases, but they can occur more frequently and be more serious. For example, special security measures used for detainees awaiting trial can be similar to measures used in other cases, but they are often on the extreme end of the scale for such measures. Attorney–client rapport issues in terrorism prosecutions are often among the most challenging. National security cases are also often among the highest in profile.

This annotated guide describes special case-management issues that typically arise in national security cases. Guide text is followed by instructive examples drawn from a selection of cases that are more fully described in a companion publication, *National Security Case Studies: Special Case-Management Challenges* (Federal Judicial Center 2011).

National Security Case Studies includes an illustrative and instructive selection of cases concerning national security issues that have appeared in Article III courts. Many of the lessons derived from these cases came from close examinations of the case files and from interviews with presiding judges—especially with respect to case-management issues that are not always written up in published opinions.

The case note headings here correspond to chapter titles in the *Case Studies*, with a few exceptions: The *Case Studies* chapter on the "First World Trade Center Bombing" includes the prosecution for the bombing itself as well as related prosecutions for a "Plot to Bomb New York City Tunnels and Landmarks" and a "Plot to Bomb U.S. Airplanes in Southeast Asia." The *Case Studies* chapter titled "Kenya and Tanzania" includes the "First Prosecution for 1998 Embassy Bombings" and a much later "Prosecution of a Guantánamo Bay Detainee for 1998 Embassy Bombings."

The electronic version of this publication appearing at FJC Online (http://cwn.fjc.dcn, on the federal judiciary's intranet) includes hyperlinks to relevant sections of the *Case Studies* and to other references. The electronic version of the publication appearing on the Internet (at http://www.fjc.gov) does not include hyperlinks.

Part I
Classified Information

Classified information is information designated by the executive branch as protected information because its unauthorized disclosure could imperil national security. Classified Information Procedures Act, 18 U.S.C. app. 3 § 1(a) (2006); Exec. Order No. 13,526 § 6.1(i), 75 Fed. Reg. 707 (Jan. 5, 2010); *see* Robert Timothy Reagan, *Keeping Government Secrets: A Pocket Guide for Judges on the State-Secrets Privilege, the Classified Information Procedures Act, and Court Security Officers* 1–3 (Federal Judicial Center 2007).

There are three levels of classification. "Confidential" information is "information, the unauthorized disclosure of which reasonably could be expected to cause damage to the national security that the original classification authority is able to identify or describe." Exec. Order No. 13,526, *supra*, § 1.2(a)(3). "Secret" information is "information, the unauthorized disclosure of which reasonably could be expected to cause *serious* damage to the national security . . . ." *Id.* § 1.2(a)(2) (emphasis added). "Top secret" information is "information, the unauthorized disclosure of which reasonably could be expected to cause *exceptionally grave* damage to the national security . . . ." *Id.* § 1.2(a)(1) (emphasis added).

The designation "confidential" is used infrequently. Most classified information presented to courts is either secret or top secret.

The executive branch allows only persons with security clearances to see or handle classified information. A security clearance is a necessary condition, but it is not a sufficient condition. The executive branch also limits access to classified information to persons whom it has determined have a "need to know."

In addition to being classified, information can be designated as "sensitive compartmented information" (SCI). Classified information that includes information about sources and methods is often "compartmented," which means that there are additional restrictions placed on access to the information, including a more restrictive requirement of need to know. Sources and methods are valuable national security resources of general application, and so they are given extra protection.

A designation of "SCI" is in addition to a designation of confidential, secret, or top secret. With respect to access, handling, and storage, the designation of SCI is effectively a designation above top secret. Information designated "secret SCI," for example, requires greater protection than top secret information that is not SCI.

The Classified Information Procedures Act

The Classified Information Procedures Act (CIPA), enacted in 1980, specifies procedures for the fair prosecution of criminal cases involving classified information. 18 U.S.C. app. 3 (2006). It does not, by its terms, apply to civil cases, but some of its provisions are often used as guidance for the handling of civil cases involving classified information.

In a terrorism prosecution, the government often has classified evidence against the defendant. The government may have additional discoverable classified information relevant to the case. In an espionage prosecution, the defendant may also have classified information relevant to the case, which the defendant may or may not contemplate introducing into evidence. These are but typical possibilities.

CIPA provides for how to incorporate classified information into a criminal case at both the discovery stage and at the trial or hearing stage. Each party has a duty to provide notice if classified information is at issue. *Id.* §§ 5(a), 6(b). Case-specific details are typically addressed at a pretrial conference:

> At any time after the filing of the indictment or information any party may move for a pretrial conference to consider matters relating to classified information that may arise in connection with the prosecution. Following such motion or on its own motion the court shall promptly hold a pretrial conference . . . .

Id. § 2.

As in any criminal case, the court may be called on to rule on whether information in the government's possession is discoverable. In a CIPA case, the court is also frequently called on to decide whether classified information in discovery can be fairly (1) omitted, (2) summarized, or (3) substituted with an admission.

> The court, upon a sufficient showing, may authorize the United States to delete specified items of classified information from documents to be made available to the defendant through discovery under the Federal Rules of Criminal Procedure, to substitute a summary of the information for such classified documents, or to substitute a statement admitting relevant facts that the classified information would tend to prove.

Id. § 4.

The court's consideration of whether to limit discovery of classified information or authorize substitutions is typically ex parte, but a record must be preserved for appeal. *Id.*

The court customarily issues a protective order requiring the defense to preserve the secrecy of classified information, and the protective order may limit what information can be shared with the defendant by defense counsel. *See id.* § 3.

At a public hearing or trial, the court may authorize the substitution for classified evidence of either (1) a summary or (2) an admission, so long as the substitution "will provide the defendant with substantially the same ability to make his defense as would disclosure of the specific classified information." *Id.* § 6(c)(1). A hearing on this issue may be conducted in camera, *id.*, and the court may receive information from the government "explaining the basis for the classification of such information" ex parte, *id.* § 6(c)(2).

Any ruling adverse to the government respecting access to classified information, including a sanction for denying access to classified information, may be resolved by expedited interlocutory appeal. *Id.* § 7.

If a fair trial necessitates the disclosure of classified information, and the government refuses to disclose the classified information, then the remedy is dismissal of the case or dismissal of one or more counts. *Id.* § 6(e).

It is also possible for the government to declassify information. This typically requires negotiation between two parts of the executive branch: the intelligence community and the prosecution. At one proceeding, the U.S. attorney observed that "the intelligence community always wants the Government to wait as long as it possibly can before it declassifies or gets substitutions because every step in that direction poses some risk of disclosure of sources, even if we do substitutions." Transcript at 16, *United States v. Ahmed*, No. 1:06-cr-147 (N.D. Ga. Sept. 18, 2008, filed Sept. 23, 2008).

CASE NOTES

Paintball

In the prosecution of Ali al-Timimi, the spiritual leader of northern Virginia men who played paintball in preparation for violent jihad, the defendant filed a CIPA motion to use classified information at trial. The judge issued a sealed protective order after a sealed CIPA hearing.

Minneapolis

Because of a plea agreement, the case against Mohamed Abdullah Warsame, who was indicted for attending Al-Qaeda training camps, never went to trial, but part of the government's case relied on classified evidence. The government was willing to declassify some of the evidence. Pursuant to CIPA, the government asked the judge to approve unclassified substitutions for other evidence. The judge compared all proposed substitutions with their corresponding originals and frequently asked for modifications.

Chicago

The prosecution of Muhammad Abdul Hamid Khalil Salah for helping to provide funds to Hamas involved a substantial amount of classified evidence. Pursuant to CIPA, the judge approved five admissions by the government as substitutions for classified evidence concerning Salah's interrogation by Israeli agents while he was in Israeli custody. For example, the government offered to admit that Israel authorized its agents to use hoods, handcuffs, and shackles during interrogations. The judge found that the substitutions were consistent with the agents' previous testimony, and Salah would be able to question the agents at trial about his specific treatment. As the trial unfolded, Salah cross-examined the agents extensively, and the vast majority of the topics covered did not involve classified information.

To explain to the jury why some topics were being skirted during examination of the witnesses, the judge prepared a jury instruction to accompany presentation of the admissions:

> This case involves certain classified information. Classified information is information or material that has been determined by the United States Government pursuant to an Executive order, statute, or regulation, to require protection against unauthorized disclosure. In lieu of disclosing specific classified information, I anticipate that you will hear certain substitutions for the classified information during this trial. These substitutions are admissions of relevant facts by the United States for purposes of this trial. The witnesses in this case as well as attorneys are prohibited from disclosing classified information and, in the case of the attorneys, are prohibited from asking questions to any witness which if answered would disclose classified information. Defendants may not cross examine a particular witness regarding the underlying classified matters set forth in these admissions. You must decide what weight, if any, to give to these admissions.

United States v. Salah, 462 F. Supp. 2d 915, 924 (N.D. Ill. 2006).

Giving State Secrets to Lobbyists

In a sting prosecution of lobbyists for sharing classified information, CIPA governed many proceedings. Pursuant to section 5(a), the defendants gave notice of their intent to introduce classified evidence at trial. Pursuant to section 6, the judge "determined that a substantial volume of the classified information was indeed relevant and admissible." *United States v. Rosen*, 557 F.3d 192, 195 (4th Cir. 2009). As permitted by section 6(c)(1), the government proposed redactions and summaries as substitutions for the classified evidence. The judge approved some of the substitutions. "In some instances, the court concluded that less extensive redactions, or the use of replacements for particular names, places, or terms, would adequately protect the defendants' rights while simultaneously offering adequate protection for classified information." *Id.* at 196.

The court of appeals heard expedited interlocutory appeals of the district judge's CIPA rules, as provided by section 7 of CIPA.

Lodi

In the prosecution of Hamid Hayat for attending a terrorist training camp, and of his father Umer for lying about it, the government filed a notice that CIPA may apply to the case because of potentially discoverable classified evidence. In the end, the only classified evidence at issue was foundational to unclassified trial evidence, and the defense attorneys were willing to stipulate to the trial evidence's admissibility.

Atlanta

In a prosecution of two young men in Atlanta for preparing for violent jihad by, among other things, making casing videos of strategic landmarks, some classified evidence had to be either declassified or substituted with court-approved summaries or admissions before it was presented at trial, and in some instances before it could be shared with defense counsel.

Classified Information Security Officers

The Department of Justice provides the courts with security experts who help the courts store and handle classified information and who help court staff and attorneys obtain security clearances.

CIPA provides for the designation of "classified information security officers," formerly and ambiguously known as "court security officers," to assist the court in keeping classified information secure.

Section 9 of CIPA calls for the Chief Justice to write procedural rules:

> Within one hundred and twenty days of the date of the enactment of this Act, the Chief Justice of the United States, in consultation with the Attorney General, the Director of National Intelligence, and the Secretary of Defense, shall prescribe rules establishing procedures for the protection against unauthorized disclosure of any classified information in the custody of the United States district courts, courts of appeal, or Supreme Court. Such rules, and any changes in such rules, shall be submitted to the appropriate committees of Congress and shall become effective forty-five days after such submission.

18 U.S.C. app. 3 § 9(a) (2006).

CIPA "Security Procedures," issued in 1981 by Chief Justice Burger and revised in 2010 by Chief Justice Roberts, specify how classified information security officers are designated:

> *2. Classified Information Security Officer.* In any proceeding in a criminal case or appeal therefrom in which classified information is within, or is reasonably expected to be within, the custody of the court, the court will designate a "classified information security officer." The Attorney General or the Department of Justice Security Officer will recommend to the court a person qualified to serve as a classified information security officer. This individual will be selected from the Litigation Security Group, Security and Emergency Planning Staff, Department of Justice, to be detailed to the court to serve in a neutral capacity. The court may designate, as required, one or more alternate classified information security officers who have been recommended in the manner specified above.

18 U.S.C. app. 3 § 9 note (2006).

The Justice Department has established a unit in its Management Division called the Litigation Security Group that consists of information security experts who are detailed to the courts. This unit is by design organizationally quite separate from the parts of the Justice Department that represent the government's interests in court cases. This unit, although expert in protecting classified information, is also separate from the intelligence community. It is to the Litigation Security Group whom courts should turn for guidance on matters relating to classified information. Although courts may be more familiar with the attorneys representing the government, it is the Litigation Security Group whose primary purpose is to provide the courts with neutral assistance. Their specific guidance is also superior to the general guidance presented here.

In a criminal case, if it is likely that the court will have to handle classified information, the Department of Justice Security Officer, who is the head of the department's Security and Emergency Planning Staff (SEPS), a unit in the Justice Management Division that includes the Litigation Security Group, recommends a security officer in the Litigation Security Group as the classified information security officer for the case. The recommendation is presented by letter to the presiding judge. Typically, the letter also recommends other security officers as alternates.

The presiding judge should appoint the security officer and alternates to the case by order. The judge may include this appointment in a protective order specifying defense attorneys' responsibilities in handling classified information. In a civil case involving classified information, the court should also contact the Litigation Security Group and appoint a classified information security officer to the case.

It is common for the security officer to deliver classified materials to the judge for in camera review. The security officer will advise the judge on security precautions for the review, such as keeping windows covered or doors closed. It is not necessary for security officers to watch a judge review classified material. Security officers generally remain available while a judge reviews classified material in private and return to the judge when the judge is finished reviewing the material.

Another important role of the security officer is to attend public proceedings in order to assist the court in preventing public disclosure of classified information.

Security Clearances for Court Staff

Article III judges are automatically cleared to see classified information necessary to the performance of their judicial function. 18 U.S.C. app. 3 § 9 note (2006); *see* Robert Timothy Reagan, *Keeping Government Secrets: A Pocket Guide for Judges on the State-Secrets Privilege, the Classified Information Procedures Act, and Court Security Officers* 3 (Federal Judicial Center 2007). Magistrate judges do not have automatic clearance, so they require a background check before they can have access to classified information. Because of the background check necessary to become a magistrate judge, this process typically takes a matter of days. Background checks for other court personnel typically take a matter of months. In some cases, interim clearances can be granted while the background investigation is under way. Only United States citizens are eligible for security clearances.

The Litigation Security Group will facilitate security clearances for court personnel. Judges in courts that frequently have cases involving classified information commonly require their law clerks to obtain security clearances. It is useful to begin the clearance process when the law clerk is hired and not wait until the law clerk begins work.

Most courts have to deal with classified information only occasionally, so it is common for court personnel to seek security clearances only when a case requiring clearances presents itself. Court personnel who already have security clearances sometimes assist with cases to which they otherwise would not be assigned. Judges sometimes decide to work on classified information without staff assistance.

Levels of security clearance relevant to the court's work usually include (1) secret, (2) top secret, or (3) TS/SCI (top secret/sensitive compartmented information). A higher security clearance requires a more extensive background check. Because it is not always possible to know with precision in advance what level of classification will be involved in a case, the Litigation Security Group customarily initiates FBI background checks on court personnel sufficiently extensive for them to be cleared at the highest level if necessary.

Access to specific classified information is limited to persons with the appropriate security clearance *and* a "need to know." Occasionally, classified information is designated for judges' eyes only, and even law clerks with high security clearances cannot see the information.

CASE NOTES

First Prosecution for 1998 Embassy Bombings

In the original prosecution for the 1998 bombings of American embassies in Kenya and Tanzania, the district judges' law clerks had security clearances. Among the judges who heard the original defendants' appeals, one judge regularly asks his law clerks to obtain security clearances, but another judge has never had a law clerk obtain one.

Millennium Bomber

In the prosecution of Ahmed Ressam, who planned to bomb the Los Angeles International Airport at the turn of the millennium, the district judge reviewed classified material to determine whether it was discoverable. The judge did this without the assistance of a law clerk, because there was not enough time for a clerk to obtain a top-secret security clearance.

Detroit

To assess the extent of prosecutorial misconduct in the first post-September 11, 2001, prosecution for terrorism, the judge had to review the prosecution's entire case file, which included extensive classified information. All of the judge's staff obtained security clearances.

Dirty Bomber

The District of South Carolina district judge assigned to consider a habeas corpus petition by Jose Padilla—originally detained as an alleged dirty bomber but later tried for terrorism conspiracy—prepared for the possibility of classified evidence in the case by having his two law clerks, his judicial assistant, a courtroom deputy, and a court reporter obtain security clearances. Because Padilla's attorneys wanted his habeas petition decided on legal grounds rather than factual grounds, classified evidence was never an important issue in the case, and it was not an issue at all during oral arguments. The judge examined some classified evidence at the court's sensitive compartmented information facility (SCIF) in Charleston, but there was no need for his staff to do so.

The Southern District of Florida district judge who heard the criminal trial of Padilla and his two codefendants also had all of her staff obtain security clearances: her law clerks, her judicial assistant, her courtroom deputy, and her court reporter. During this case, the judge did not use interns, because they would not have security clearances.

Minneapolis

In the prosecution of Mohamed Abdullah Warsame for attending Al-Qaeda training camps, the district judge's staff obtained security clearances. The district judge presided over pretrial matters that would ordinarily go to a magistrate judge so that another chambers' staff would not have to obtain security clearances.

Detainee Documents

The Southern District of New York judge who heard a Freedom of Information Act case concerning extraterritorial detentions of terrorism suspects has all of his law clerks obtain security clearances. The clerks begin the process of obtaining clearances before they start work.

Prosecution of a Charity

The prosecution of the Holy Land Foundation and its principals for providing funds to Hamas required two trials because of a hung jury after the first one. Law clerks and other staff members for the judges presiding over both trials received security clearances.

Chicago

For a prosecution of Muhammad Abdul Hamid Khalil Salah for helping to provide funds to Hamas—a trial that involved a substantial amount of classified evidence relating to Salah's imprisonment in Israel—the judge's law clerks sought security clearances. Because the clearance process took a substantial fraction of the law clerks' tenure, the judge handled classified issues without law clerk assistance. It was necessary, however, for a court reporter working on the case to have a security clearance.

Giving State Secrets to Lobbyists

The judge who presided over a sting prosecution of lobbyists for sharing classified information has a career law clerk with a security clearance. One of the judge's temporary law clerks during the time of this case, however, was a Canadian citizen, so he was not eligible for a security clearance.

Lodi

For the prosecution of Hamid Hayat for attending a terrorist training camp, and of his father Umer for lying about it, the presiding judge's court reporter obtained a security clearance, and as a backup precaution another court reporter at the courthouse did as well.

Warrantless Wiretaps

In actions challenging a secret and allegedly illegal surveillance program by the National Security Agency, all classified information presented to the court was designated by the government as for judges' eyes only, and not even law clerks with security clearances were permitted to see it.

Atlanta

In a prosecution of two young men in Atlanta for preparing for violent jihad by, among other things, making casing videos of strategic landmarks, court staff had to obtain security clearances. This included magistrate judges, who do not have the same automatic security clearances as Article III judges.

Fort Dix

In a prosecution of six men for conspiracy to attack Fort Dix, all of the judge's staff—law clerks, court reporters, courtroom deputies, and the judicial assistant—received security clearances. The judge observed that the clearance process went smoothly.

Security Clearances for Attorneys

If classified information is at least discoverable in a criminal case, it is customary for the defendant's attorneys to have security clearances. In districts in which such cases are common, there may be local criminal defense attorneys who already have security clearances. Often, the case at hand is an attorney's first need for a clearance.

The Litigation Security Group can facilitate security clearances as needed for defense attorneys and for persons working with defense attorneys, such as paralegals and investigators. It is customary for obligations to preserve the secrecy of classified information to be specified in a protective order signed by the judge and in a memorandum of understanding signed by the persons granted clearance.

The Federal Judicial Center has assembled a selection of protective orders used in national security cases: *National Security Prosecutions: Protective Orders*. Judges should consult the classified information security officer when drafting national security protective orders.

In some cases, an attorney may be denied a security clearance or the attorney may decline to seek one. The court might replace the attorney unless there is another cleared attorney on the defense team, or the court might make a special appointment of a cleared attorney to work on issues in the case pertaining to classified information.

The Litigation Security Group can also facilitate security clearances for attorneys in civil cases, including habeas corpus cases. The government's willingness to actually grant plaintiffs' attorneys access to classified information in civil cases challenging the government depends on the circumstances of the case.

In any case involving classified information, it is often useful for the judge to meet jointly with attorneys and the classified information security officer early in the case.

CASE NOTES

First Prosecution for 1998 Embassy Bombings

In the original prosecution for the 1998 bombings of American embassies in Kenya and Tanzania, defense counsel had to have security clearances in order to have access to classified evidence. The court of appeals affirmed a district judge's ruling that requiring security clearances for defense attorneys did not violate their clients' Sixth Amendment rights. *In re Terrorist Bombings of U.S. Embassies in East Africa*, 552 F.3d 93, 119–28 (2d Cir. 2008); *see United States v. Bin Laden*, 58 F. Supp. 2d 113 (S.D.N.Y. 1999).

Would-Be Spy

In the prosecution of Brian Patrick Regan for attempted espionage, defense attorneys had security clearances, and the defendant himself was cleared to see some classified information related to the information he was accused of trying to sell. *United States v. Regan*, 281 F. Supp. 2d 795, 801 (E.D. Va. 2002).

Detroit

An assessment of prosecutorial misconduct in the first post-September 11, 2001, prosecution for terrorism required review of the prosecution's entire case file, which included extensive classified information. Defense attorneys were required to obtain security clearances.

The district judge in this case recommends that a judge in a case that might include classified information meet early with attorneys to discuss how much classified information is at issue and who will need security clearances. It is important to establish contact with the Litigation Security Group as soon as it is known that the case might involve classified information.

Twentieth Hijacker

In the prosecution of Zacarias Moussaoui for terrorism conspiracy, the defendant's attorneys obtained security clearances and signed a memorandum of understanding requiring that classified secrets be kept secret forever. *United States v. Moussaoui, 591 F.3d 263, 267 (4th Cir. 2010).

Guantánamo Bay

Habeas attorneys representing Guantánamo Bay detainees needed security clearances to visit their clients.

Among the Guantánamo Bay detainees who filed habeas corpus petitions was Abu Zubaydah, a senior Al-Qaeda figure who was treated for frequent seizures. The district court ordered the government to grant Abu Zubaydah's attorneys, who had security clearances, access to his medical records so that they could investigate whether side effects from medical treatment at Guantánamo Bay were interfering with his ability to communicate effectively with his attorneys, despite the government's initial determination that portions would be redacted for lack of a need to know.

Dirty Bomber

In the trial of Jose Padilla, originally detained as a dirty bomber but ultimately tried with two other men for terrorism conspiracy, all defense attorneys received security clearances.

A Plot to Kill President Bush

In the prosecution of Ahmed Omar Abu Ali for terrorism conspiracy and conspiracy to kill the President, some of the evidence against the defendant was classified. One of the defendant's attorneys was denied a security clearance and the other did not apply for one, so the court appointed an attorney who already had a clearance. *United States v. Abu Ali*, 528 F.3d 210, 248–49 (4th Cir. 2008). Only the cleared attorney, and not the defendant or either uncleared attorney, was allowed to see classified evidence or participate in hearings in which classified evidence was discussed.

Paintball

On appeal from the conviction of Ali al-Timimi, the spiritual leader of northern Virginia men who played paintball in preparation for violent jihad, the court of appeals remanded the case for an investigation of possibly discoverable surveillance. On remand, the government presented to the judge classified submissions that neither the prosecuting nor the defense attorneys were cleared to see. The judge issued an order that her law clerk and the attorneys be granted clearance to examine at least some of the secret submissions.

Minneapolis

In the prosecution of Mohamed Abdullah Warsame for attending Al-Qaeda training camps, the defendant's attorneys obtained security clearances. The court initially appointed the federal defender's office to represent Warsame. The defendant's supporters, however, thought that retained counsel would provide better representation, so they hired a law professor in Chicago to represent Warsame. Because the professor could not identify local counsel likely to obtain a security clearance, the court kept the federal defender's office as second counsel.

Prosecution of a Charity

In the prosecution of the Holy Land Foundation and its principals for providing funds to Hamas, defense attorneys received security clearances.

Chicago

In the prosecution of Muhammad Abdul Hamid Khalil Salah for helping to provide funds to Hamas—a prosecution that involved a substantial amount of classified evidence relating to Salah's imprisonment in Israel—defense counsel elected not to seek security clearances, so the judge resolved evidentiary issues by holding ex parte conferences with defense counsel to determine their defense needs and ex parte conferences with government counsel to determine what classified information the government held.

Giving State Secrets to Lobbyists

In a sting prosecution of lobbyists for sharing classified information, defense attorneys had security clearances, and some witnesses for the defense also had security clearances.

Lodi

In the Sacramento prosecution of Hamid Hayat for attending a terrorist training camp, and of his father Umer for lying about it, the government filed a notice that it had potentially discoverable classified evidence. Defense attorneys did not want to obtain security clearances, so the judge looked for other local attorneys who already had clearances. The classified information security officer could not find a local defense attorney with a security clearance, but he was able to identify two in a neighboring district who were cleared. Because the defendants were willing to stipulate to the admissibility of trial evidence that had classified information as part of its foundation, having cleared counsel ultimately was not necessary.

Warrantless Wiretaps

In an action challenging a secret and allegedly illegal surveillance program—an action arising from evidence of surveillance in a top-secret document mistakenly disclosed to an Islamic charity during proceedings to freeze the charity's assets for allegedly funding terrorism—the plaintiffs were required to surrender all copies of the document, and they were forbidden by the government from having access to the copy they delivered to the court. *Al-Haramain Islamic Found. v. Bush*, 451 F. Supp. 2d 1215, 1217, 1229 (D. Or. 2006).

Attorneys representing the government told the court that they were not at liberty to disclose whether or not they had clearance to see the document.

The action was consolidated with other actions, for pretrial purposes, by the Judicial Panel on Multidistrict Litigation, and the transferee judge ordered the government to give the plaintiffs' attorneys security clearances and access to the document. *In re NSA Telecomm. Records Litig.*, 595 F. Supp. 2d 1077, 1089–90 (N.D. Cal. 2009). Two attorneys for the plaintiffs received security clearances, but the government decided that pursuing the action against the government was not a sufficient "need to know" required for access to the document.

Atlanta

In a prosecution of two young men in Atlanta for preparing for violent jihad by, among other things, making casing videos of strategic landmarks, defense attorneys had to obtain security clearances.

Fort Dix

In a prosecution of six men for conspiracy to attack Fort Dix, the defense attorneys needed security clearances.

Handling and Storing Classified Information

Courts and attorneys for parties other than the federal government must rely on the Litigation Security Group for guidance on handling and storing classified information. Following are summary guidelines, but the classified information security officers provided by the Litigation Security Group are the experts.

Security requirements for classified information depend on the level of classification. A person handling classified information must have a security clearance at least as high as the information's level of classification. Handling classified information includes not only reviewing it but also carrying it from a place of storage to a judge for review. A person handling top secret information, for example, must have at least a top secret security clearance, but only a secret security clearance is required to handle secret information. A TS/SCI security clearance is required to review SCI (sensitive compartmented information). In addition, access to classified information will be restricted to persons who "need to know."

Classified information must not be reviewed in the presence of persons without an appropriate security clearance and must never be reviewed in public.

Classified documents are marked with the applicable level of classification. Each paragraph of a classified document should be marked with the level of classification for the paragraph: (U) for unclassified, (C) for confidential, (S) for secret, (TS) for top secret, and (TS/SCI) for top secret/sensitive compartmented information. The level of classification for a document is the highest level of classification among its parts.

Confidential, secret, and top secret material must be stored in an approved safe in a secure room. The classified information security officer will provide a suitable safe and will work with the court to identify or help establish a suitable room. Judges presiding over cases involving classified information typically keep a safe suitable for storing classified materials in their chambers. If defense attorneys need to review classified materials, the court and the classified information security officer typically identify a secure room for this purpose and establish a safe to store the materials.

SCI must be stored in a sensitive compartmented information facility (SCIF). A SCIF (customarily pronounced "skiff") is a room, sometimes a building, that meets certain security specifications, such as slab-to-slab construction, special locks, and an alarm system connected to armed security guards. If a courthouse does not already have a SCIF, and it is determined that one is needed at the courthouse, then the classified information security officer will establish one, at the executive branch's expense. 18 U.S.C. app. 3 § 9 note ¶ 12 (2006). Alternatively, the classified information security officer can often locate a SCIF nearby for the court's use.

U.S. attorney offices and FBI offices often have SCIFs. Although judges sometimes express reluctance to use these for the court's work, the classified information security officer can establish protective measures suitably limiting access to stored materials. If classified materials are stored in a SCIF for use by the court or a party opposing the government, and the SCIF is not under the court's control, then the materials will be stored within the SCIF in a way that permits only the classified information security officer and the judge or attorney, as the case may be, to have access to the materials. Designated safes or locked bags are often used for this purpose.

Any document based on classified information, such as notes, briefs, and opinions, may be classified at the highest level of classification of the material on which the document is based. Storage requirements for the derivative document, therefore, may be the same as the storage requirements for the classified material on which it is based. Typically, the classified information security officer coordinates a security review to determine the level of classification, if any, for a derivative document.

Classified information cannot be discussed or transmitted by email or over a non-secure telephone line.

Court personnel with security clearances may transport classified material from the place of storage to the place of review for a judge or other persons.

CASE NOTES

Plot to Bomb New York City Tunnels and Landmarks

In the prosecution for a conspiracy to bomb New York tunnels and landmarks, the government presented six classified exhibits ex parte to the district judge, pursuant to CIPA. *United States v. Rahman*, 870 F. Supp. 47, 49 (S.D.N.Y. 1994). The judge kept the exhibits in a safe while he considered whether they had to be produced to the defense. He ruled which exhibit had to be disclosed to the defense, ordered that it not be disclosed to anyone else, and ordered that all of the exhibits be kept under seal with the classified information security officer.

Millennium Bomber

In the prosecution of Ahmed Ressam, who planned to bomb the Los Angeles International Airport at the turn of the millennium, the district judge reviewed classified materials to determine whether the materials were discoverable. The judge kept the materials in a safe to which the classified information security officer, but not the judge, had access. The judge preferred not to have to deal with the lock and combination himself.

Would-Be Spy

In the prosecution of Brian Patrick Regan for attempted espionage, the government discovered in the defendant's jail cell what appeared to be coded messages to his wife and children concerning the locations of hidden information. *United States v. Regan*, 281 F. Supp. 2d 795, 800, 804–05, 807 (E.D. Va. 2002). The government wanted to search the defense SCIF to look for evidence that the documents were improperly created on a computer there. The district judge did not allow the U.S. Attorney's Office or the FBI to conduct the search; instead, he authorized the classified information security officers to conduct the search.

Detroit

An assessment of prosecutorial misconduct in the first post-September 11, 2001, prosecution for terrorism required review of the prosecution's entire case file, which included extensive classified information. Classified information security officers created a SCIF in the courthouse. Only chambers staff with security clearances could enter this SCIF.

The judge also had to review extensive highly sensitive records maintained at CIA headquarters. He negotiated with the CIA's general counsel to establish a protocol for use of the CIA's evidence. Because many of the CIA records were too sensitive to transport to Michigan, the judge traveled to Virginia to review them.

American Taliban

In the prosecution of John Walker Lindh, who became known as the American Taliban, the government's classified evidence that the district judge reviewed for discoverability was stored in the court's SCIF. The judge's law clerks typically obtain security clearances, and classified materials are kept within eyesight at all times.

September 11 Damages

In the consolidated civil actions against alleged supporters of the September 11, 2001, attacks, plaintiffs supported a discovery motion with anonymously leaked documents that the plaintiffs knew were sensitive and suspected might be classified. The attorneys delivered the documents to the court, sent copies to the U.S. attorney, and provided defendants with only a copy of the transmittal letter. The government determined that at least some of the documents were classified, so the court's copies were securely stored. The plaintiffs were required to surrender their copies of the documents.

Guantánamo Bay

After news media reported that classified information about Guantánamo Bay detainees became available on the Internet as a result of unauthorized disclosures to WikiLeaks, cleared habeas attorneys for the detainees were admonished not to allow their knowledge of properly disclosed classified information to provide clues, by words or by actions, as to the authenticity of any leaked purportedly classified information.

Dirty Bomber

In the trial of Jose Padilla—who was originally detained as a dirty bomber but ultimately tried with two other men for terrorism conspiracy—classified information was reviewed by defense attorneys in the court's basement SCIF. Both the judge and the defense attorneys viewed classified videos of interrogations of Padilla conducted while he was in military detention.

The judge reviewed, as provided by CIPA, an evidentiary substitute for classified evidence. An agent of the intelligence agency with authority over the evidence brought the original evidence to the classified information security officer, who delivered it to the judge in chambers for her private review in her office while the agent and the security officer waited outside her door.

A Plot to Kill President Bush

In the prosecution of Ahmed Omar Abu Ali for terrorism conspiracy and conspiracy to kill the President, classified evidence was stored in the court's SCIF.

Minneapolis

The case against Mohamed Abdullah Warsame, who was prosecuted for attending Al-Qaeda training camps, relied on classified evidence. Early in the case, the government produced to defense counsel discoverable classified evidence, and the attorneys reviewed the classified material in a secure room at the courthouse, which included a safe suitable for storing classified materials. The attorneys had to prepare any documents based on or referring to classified material in the secure room. The court reporter, who had a security clearance, also had to work on transcripts containing classified information in this room and store computer equipment she used for such transcripts in the safe. The judge could keep classified materials in a safe in his chambers office.

Mistaken Rendition

Relying on a classified declaration presented for the judge's eyes only, the district court dismissed a complaint, on state-secrets grounds, alleging that the CIA abducted and imprisoned Khaled el-Masri until it realized that it had picked up the wrong person. *El-Masri v. Tenet*, 437 F. Supp. 2d 530 (E.D. Va. 2006), *aff'd*, 479 F.3d 296 (4th Cir. 2007). The classified declaration was delivered to the judge by a classified information security officer, who took responsibility for storing the declaration when the judge was not privately reviewing it.

Prosecution of a Charity

The prosecution of the Holy Land Foundation and its principals for providing funds to Hamas was based in part on classified evidence, including information obtained under the Foreign Intelligence Surveillance Act and information provided by the government of Israel. A second trial was required because of a hung jury after the first one. The judges presiding over the two trials each kept classified documents in a chambers safe. The court found space that could be fitted as a secure room for defense counsel to store and review classified documents; a separate safe was established for each defendant.

Chicago

For the prosecution of Muhammad Abdul Hamid Khalil Salah for helping to provide funds to Hamas, the judge kept classified materials in a chambers safe to which only the judge and a cleared court reporter had the combination. For hearings concerning classified documents, the court reporter used a laptop provided by classified information security officers; the laptop was also stored in the safe.

To ensure against surveillance of proceedings by enemies, deputy marshals electronically monitored conferences and hearings in which classified information was discussed.

Giving State Secrets to Lobbyists

For a sting prosecution of lobbyists for sharing classified information, defense attorneys with security clearances reviewed classified evidence in a courthouse SCIF designed for use by criminal defense counsel. Defense witnesses with security clearances could also review classified information in the SCIF, but they were required to do so after usual operating hours.

Warrantless Wiretaps

Lawyers for an Islamic charity that the government shut down for allegedly funding terrorism filed an action in Portland, Oregon, against a secret and allegedly illegal surveillance program. The lawyers submitted as evidence of the surveillance a top-secret document mistakenly disclosed to the charity during proceedings to freeze the charity's assets. After the classified document had remained in a sealed envelope in the judge's chambers for two weeks, a government security officer reviewed it in chambers and determined that it contained sensitive compartmented information, which meant it had to be stored in a SCIF. The courthouse did not have a SCIF. The FBI had a SCIF in Portland, but the FBI was a party to the case, so the plaintiffs did not want the document stored there. It was agreed that the document would be sent to the Seattle U.S. attorney's SCIF. Shortly thereafter, the plaintiffs agreed to a method of storage at the FBI's Portland SCIF: the document was stored in a locked bag to which only the judge and a classified information security officer would have a key. *Al-Haramain Islamic*

Found. v. Bush, 451 F. Supp. 2d 1215, 1219 (D. Or. 2006).

The government required the plaintiffs and their attorneys to surrender all copies of the document. The attorneys said that they complied with the government's instructions, but the attorneys said that they could not comment on whether their clients had done so without violating the attorney–client privilege. The government made no effort to retrieve any copies of the document that may have been sent abroad, and it was reported that a reporter for the *Washington Post* had reviewed the document.

The district judge ruled that the plaintiffs could rely on their memories of the classified document to support their case, but the court of appeals determined that if they could not rely on the document itself then neither could they rely on their memories of it. *Al-Haramain Islamic Found. v. Bush*, 507 F.3d 1190, 1203 (9th Cir. 2007).

In a related action under the Freedom of Information Act (FOIA), the judge spent many hours over several days reviewing claimed exemptions in camera and ex parte. The government would not allow even law clerks with security clearances to assist the judge in this review. Doors were closed, windows were covered, and the documents were under the judge's immediate control at all times. The documents were not stored in chambers; classified information security officers, whose offices and storage facilities, at the time, were a few blocks away from the federal courthouse in the District of Columbia, delivered and retrieved the documents on request.

Another judge presiding over another related FOIA action adopted a procedure for ensuring an accurate appellate record: he initialed and dated any classified document he reviewed that was not kept in the court's file.

A judge hearing another related action prepared a sealed ex parte opinion responding to classified ex parte government submissions. *See Terkel v. AT&T*, 441 F. Supp. 2d 899, 902 (N.D. Ill. 2006). To write the classified opinion, the judge used a laptop computer provided by the classified information security officer. The computer, and all drafts of the opinion, were stored in the U.S. attorney's SCIF in the same building.

Atlanta

In a prosecution of two young men in Atlanta for preparing for violent jihad by, among other things, making casing videos of strategic landmarks, some classified information in the case was designated SCI. Judges and court staff could view this information at the U.S. attorney's SCIF in the same building as the courthouse.

Some classified information in the case was not SCI, and judges could store this in chambers safes. A secure room was set aside for defense counsel to store and review classified information.

Sears Tower

Not all national security cases involve classified information. The prosecution of the "Liberty City Seven" for conspiracy to topple the Sears Tower and attack other buildings in various cities, based on information provided by paid informants, involved no classified information.

Fort Dix

In a prosecution of six men for conspiracy to attack Fort Dix, defense attorneys, who had security clearances, reviewed classified materials in a secure room in the courthouse; a separate safe was designated for each defendant. The attorneys did not have to see SCI, but the judge did. A classified information security officer brought the SCI to the judge's chambers and took it away when the judge was finished examining it.

Torture Flights

In a tort action pertaining to extraordinary rendition, the government supported a successful motion to dismiss on state-secrets grounds with a classified ex parte declaration by the head of the CIA. A classified information security officer brought the declaration to the district judge's chambers. The judge reviewed the declaration privately in his office, with the blinds drawn, while the security officer waited outside. When the judge was finished reviewing the declaration, the security officer took it back and informed the judge that it could be brought back to him for another review at any time.

Sharing Classified Information with Criminal Defendants

Courts have found it proper for the government to share classified information with defense attorneys who have security clearances even if the attorneys cannot share the information with their clients. Protective orders prohibit counsel from sharing the information with unauthorized persons. It has been held improper, however, to deny the defendant access to classified information entered into evidence at the defendant's criminal trial. *United States v. Abu Ali*, 528 F.3d 210, 248–55 (4th Cir. 2008).

CASE NOTES

First Prosecution for 1998 Embassy Bombings

In the original prosecution for the 1998 bombings of American embassies in Kenya and Tanzania, defense counsel could not discuss classified evidence with their clients. The court of appeals affirmed the district judge's determination that this did not violate the Constitution. *In re Terrorist Bombings of U.S. Embassies in East Africa*, 552 F.3d 93, 116–23 (2d Cir. 2008).

Twentieth Hijacker

Attorneys representing Zacarias Moussaoui, in his trial for terrorism conspiracy, had security clearances, but they could not share classified information with the defendant. *United States v. Moussaoui*, 591 F.3d 263, 607 (4th Cir. 2010). Moussaoui pleaded guilty against his attorneys' advice and sought to rescind his guilty plea after the jury spared his life. *Id.* at 272, 278; *United States v. Moussaoui*, 483 F.3d 220, 223–24 n.1 (4th Cir. 2007). On appeal, his attorneys argued that their client would not have pleaded guilty if he had access to some of the classified information concerning the case that the attorneys had access to. *Moussaoui*, 591 F.3d at 272. The court of appeals affirmed the district court's denial of this request: "Moussaoui was well aware that there was classified, exculpatory evidence yet to be produced to him personally *and* he knew why the material was exculpatory. Rather than wait for the process to be completed, Moussaoui made the strategic decision to plead guilty immediately." *Id.* at 287.

Guantánamo Bay

Habeas attorneys could not share classified information with Guantánamo Bay detainees, except for the detainees' own statements made to government agents.

Dirty Bomber

More than two years after Jose Padilla—who originally was detained as a dirty bomber but was ultimately tried with two other men for terrorism conspiracy—was added to the indictment, the district judge granted him access to classified evidence created during his military detention. Although it is common to grant defense attorneys access to classified evidence relevant to a prosecution, it is very unusual for courts to grant such access to terrorism defendants.

A Plot to Kill President Bush

In the prosecution of Ahmed Omar Abu Ali for terrorism conspiracy and conspiracy to kill the President, some of the evidence against the defendant was classified, and the defendant was not allowed to see it. A small amount of classified information was presented to the jury at trial but not shown to the defendant; the court of appeals determined that this was error. *United States v. Abu Ali*, 528 F.3d 210, 248–55 (4th Cir. 2008). The court determined, however, that the error was harmless in this case.

Prosecution of a Charity

For the prosecution of the Holy Land Foundation and its principals for providing funds to Hamas, defense attorneys had security clearances, but they were not allowed to reveal classified information to their clients.

Fort Dix

In a prosecution for conspiracy to attack Fort Dix, defense attorneys had security clearances, and they had to examine classified materials, but they were not permitted to share classified information with their clients.

Discovery

In criminal cases involving classified information, the court must often not only decide what information in the government's possession is discoverable, but, pursuant to CIPA, 18 U.S.C. app. 3 § 4 (2006), must decide whether the government can substitute summaries or admissions for the original classified information. These cases frequently present "a conflict raising vitally important interests to both parties—the government's interest in protecting national security through the non-disclosure of classified information, on the one hand, and the defendant's need to acquire this information to present an adequate defense, on the other." Reggie B. Walton, *Prosecuting International Terrorism Cases in Article III Courts*, 39 Geo. L.J. Ann. Rev. Crim. Proc. iii, iii (2010).

Security precautions are required for the court's review of classified information for discovery obligations. Classified information must not be reviewed in the presence of anyone without the appropriate security clearance. A law clerk may assist the judge only if the law clerk is granted a security clearance to do so. If the matter is delegated to a magistrate judge, the magistrate judge will have to be cleared first. Classified material must be properly stored when it is not being reviewed.

Sometimes, the government can declassify information to facilitate a prosecution. This typically requires negotiation between the prosecutors and the intelligence community. Because of the secrecy associated with classified information, the prosecutors may not be immediately aware of all discoverable information in the government's possession.

Determining what information in the government's possession might be helpful to the defense is often even more difficult in a case involving classified information than it is in other criminal cases. Some judges have ex parte conversations with the defense to learn defense strategies and ex parte conversations with the prosecution to learn what information the government has in order to better understand what classified information in the government's possession might be helpful to the defense.

CASE NOTES

First Prosecution for 1998 Embassy Bombings

In the original prosecution for the 1998 bombings of American embassies in Kenya and Tanzania, the district judge resolved issues concerning discovery of classified information by conducting ex parte discussions with defense counsel concerning defense strategy and ex parte discussions with prosecutors concerning potentially relevant classified information. Sometimes, the judge was able to mediate a substitution for classified information. *In re Terrorist Bombings of U.S. Embassies in East Africa*, 552 F.3d 93, 118–19 (2d Cir. 2008). Sometimes, the judge was able to determine that classified information was not as relevant as defense counsel thought it might be.

Prosecution of a Guantánamo Bay Detainee for 1998 Embassy Bombings

In preparation for the 2010 trial of Ahmed Khalfan Ghailani, a onetime fugitive, the district judge reviewed classified CIA reports containing statements made by the defendant during custodial interrogations. The judge determined that defense counsel were entitled to additional information about the time and circumstances of the defendants' statements.

Millennium Bomber

In the prosecution of Ahmed Ressam, who planned to bomb the Los Angeles International Airport at the turn of the millennium, the district judge reviewed classified material to determine whether it was discoverable, and he decided that it was not.

American Taliban

In the prosecution of John Walker Lindh, who became known as the American Taliban, the district judge had to review a substantial amount of classified material to determine what evidence the government had to produce to the defense.

Paintball

In the prosecution of Ali al-Timimi, the spiritual leader of northern Virginia men who played paintball in preparation for violent jihad, it was difficult for the court to determine whether the defendant had been provided with all discoverable information, because prosecutors did not necessarily have access to classified information held by other parts of the government.

Lodi

In the Sacramento prosecution of Hamid Hayat for attending a terrorist training camp, and of his father Umer for lying about it, the government filed a notice that it had potentially discoverable classified evidence. After several sealed ex parte in camera reviews and hearings, the judge determined that classified information foundational to trial evidence was discoverable. Defense counsel elected to stipulate to the admissibility of the trial evidence rather than undergo the burden and delay of security clearance procedures.

FISA Evidence

The Foreign Intelligence Surveillance Act (FISA), 50 U.S.C. §§ 1801–1885c (2006), requires the government to obtain a warrant for surveillance of international communications that include a person in the United States. *See* 2 James G. Carr & Patricia L. Bellia, The Law of Electronic Surveillance 429–86 (2011); Reggie B. Walton, *Prosecuting International Terrorism Cases in Article III Courts*, 39 Geo. L.J. Ann. Rev. Crim. Proc. iii, xvi–xxiv (2010).

FISA warrants are issued by a special FISA court, whose proceedings are conducted ex parte and in secret. 50 U.S.C. § 1803 (2006). The FISA court can also issue warrants for physical searches within the United States for the purpose of obtaining foreign intelligence. *Id.* § 1822.

If the prosecution believes that it will rely on evidence obtained because of a FISA warrant, then the court may be called upon to review the warrant application to determine whether the evidence was properly obtained pursuant to a properly issued warrant. The defense is not typically granted access to materials in the warrant application. On the one hand, the court must review the collection of FISA evidence without the benefit of adverse counsel; on the other hand, the review has the benefit of previous scrutiny by another judge.

CASE NOTES

Dirty Bomber

In the trial of Jose Padilla—who was originally detained as a dirty bomber but ultimately tried with two other men for terrorism conspiracy—some of the evidence against each of the defendants resulted from warrants issued by the FISA court. Challenges to this evidence necessitated the court's review of the FISA warrant applications. The district judge referred the matter to a magistrate judge, who reviewed in camera all relevant FISA applications. After her own careful review, the district judge affirmed the magistrate judge's findings of proper probable cause for all applications.

Minneapolis

In the prosecution of Mohamed Abdullah Warsame, who was indicted for attending Al-Qaeda training camps, some of the evidence against the defendant was obtained as a result of FISA warrants. *United States v. Warsame*, 547 F. Supp. 2d 982, 984–86 (D. Minn. 2008). The FISA court had issued warrants for surveillance of persons with whom Warsame communicated, and later the court approved a tap of Warsame's telephone and a physical search of his apartment. The district judge presiding over the prosecution reviewed all warrant applications and supporting materials in camera, making de novo judgments as to probable cause, and determined that FISA procedures were properly followed.

Prosecution of a Charity

The prosecution of the Holy Land Foundation and its principals for providing funds to Hamas was based in part on wiretaps authorized by the FISA court. In discovery, the government produced FISA evidence to defense counsel, who had security clearances but who could not disclose classified information to their clients. Much of this evidence was in the form of declassified "tech-cuts," which are English-language summaries of recorded conversations. Defense counsel discovered some errors in the summaries, and the judge declared the errors to be "disturbing," but the defendants did not present evidence of sufficient inaccuracies to require a remedy.

In error, the government also disclosed to defense counsel the contents of some FISA warrant applications. This is not the usual procedure for affording a defendant an opportunity to challenge evidence based on FISA warrants. The usual procedure is for the government to present the FISA warrant records to the district judge ex parte. In fact, the judge spent several days conducting an in camera review of FISA warrants resulting in evidence the government sought to use in the case.

The judge was at a conference in another city when he received, in the lobby of his hotel, an emergency motion from the FBI stating that FISA applications had been inadvertently disclosed to defense attorneys. The FBI asked the judge for relief because the attorneys refused to return them. The judge issued an order preserving the status quo and then ultimately granted the FBI substantially the relief requested.

The government declassified some of the defendants' recorded conversations, and that evidence could be shared with the defendants. The court approved an offer by the government to seek declassification of additional conversations specifically identified by the defendants. Defense counsel argued that the offer was unconstitutional because it required them to reveal too much about their own conversations with their clients and their trial strategy. The judge overruled this objection.

It was understood that any FISA evidence the government presented at trial would have to be declassified and provided to the individual defendants in advance of trial.

Toledo

In a prosecution of Americans for conspiracy to fight against U.S. forces in Iraq, the district judge determined that it was not necessary to disclose to defense counsel FISA application materials; the court would determine the validity of the FISA evidence ex parte and in camera. *United States v. Amawi*, 531 F. Supp. 2d 832 (N.D. Ohio 2008).

Atlanta

In a prosecution of two young men in Atlanta for preparing for violent jihad by, among other things, making casing videos of strategic landmarks, some evidence against the defendants was obtained pursuant to FISA warrants. The magistrate judge reviewed all relevant FISA applications, finding no errors in FISA procedures and finding that none of the FISA materials were discoverable. The judge observed that defense counsel is in a difficult position when arguing for suppression of FISA evidence, because they do not have access to the FISA records, but a FISA suppression motion is easier for the judge than many other suppression motions because collection of the FISA evidence has been subjected to prior judicial review.

Fort Dix

In a prosecution for conspiracy to attack Fort Dix, much of the evidence against the defendants had been obtained with FISA warrants. The judge reviewed FISA files to determine what was discoverable and to determine that the FISA surveillance was properly supported.

Much of the FISA evidence was declassified, but the affidavits supporting the FISA warrants generally were not. The judge observed that FISA discoverability decisions are somewhat hampered by the judge's not knowing, particularly early in the case, what the defenses might be.

Civil Cases

Civil actions involving classified information include actions arising from contracts, torts, habeas corpus, and the Freedom of Information Act (FOIA). Typically, the government either is a defendant or it has interests aligned with a defendant. That means that the incentive structure for sharing classified information with the government's opposing party is quite different. In a criminal case, the government has an incentive to share classified information, such as by declassifying it or granting defense attorneys security clearances to see it. In a civil case, the government's goal is often to have the case dismissed. An interesting exception arose in habeas actions pertaining to detention at Guantánamo Bay, in which the district court imposed on the government the burden of proof.

CASE NOTES

Burma

In an action by the Drug Enforcement Administration's attaché in Burma claiming illegal surveillance, the district court determined that CIPA, which technically applies only to criminal cases, would apply to classified evidence in this civil case.

The district judge also overruled a government determination that attorneys in the case did not have a need to know classified information. The Litigation Security Group determined that the attorneys were eligible for security clearances, but the government declined to acknowledge their need to know classified information that was actually already known to them.

Guantánamo Bay

Habeas actions by Guantánamo Bay detainees are technically civil actions, but the district court for the District of Columbia determined that the security principles of CIPA apply to these cases.

Mistaken Rendition

A court of appeals affirmed a district court's dismissal on state-secrets grounds of a tort action arising from extraordinary rendition involving mistaken identity. *El-Masri v. United States*, 479 F.3d 296 (4th Cir. 2007).

Detainee Documents

A district court reviewed government information about terrorism suspects detained at extraterritorial military facilities since September 11, 2001, to determine what must be produced pursuant to FOIA requests. *E.g.*, *ACLU v. Dep't of Defense*, 723 F. Supp. 2d 621 (S.D.N.Y. 2010).

Warrantless Wiretaps

In an action challenging a secret and allegedly illegal surveillance program—an action arising from evidence of surveillance in a top-secret document mistakenly disclosed to an Islamic charity during proceedings to freeze the charity's assets for allegedly funding terrorism—the district judge was able to resolve the case in the plaintiffs' favor without use of the classified document. The government had publicly acknowledged surveillance of the charity and presented to the court no warrant for doing so. *In re NSA Telecomm. Records Litig.*, 700 F. Supp. 2d 1182 (N.D. Cal. 2010).

In a related FOIA action, the classified status of opinions concerning the surveillance program prepared by the Justice Department's Office of Legal Counsel (OLC) changed during the course of litigation, so the government agreed to the plaintiffs' demand that the government review again its position on whether the opinions or parts of them could be produced.

Torture Flights

A court of appeals affirmed a district court's dismissal on state-secrets grounds of a tort action pertaining to extraordinary rendition. *Mohamed v. Jeppesen Dataplan, Inc.*, 614 F.3d 1070 (9th Cir. 2010).

Other Government Secrets

Not all sensitive government information is classified. Exec. Order No. 13,556, 75 Fed. Reg. 68,675 (Nov. 9, 2010) (concerning controlled unclassified information). The government will sometimes ask the court to issue protective orders and seal part of the court record to protect sensitive information, and the court may look to the law of sealing for guidance. *See* Robert Timothy Reagan, *Sealing Court Records and Proceedings: A Pocket Guide* (Federal Judicial Center 2010).

CASE NOTES

American Taliban

In the prosecution of John Walker Lindh, who became known as the American Taliban, the government determined that it had to disclose to the defense information that was not classified but that nevertheless required sensitive handling for the benefit of national security: "reports of interviews of detainees captured in Afghanistan and elsewhere who may have knowledge of al Qaeda or who may have been members of that organization and who are housed primarily at Guantánamo Bay, Cuba." *United States v. Lindh*, 198 F. Supp. 2d 739, 741 (E.D. Va. 2002).

The district judge approved redactions to the discovery, such as agent and case identifiers. The judge also issued a protective order requiring that defense personnel given access to the discovery preserve its secrecy. The defense agreed to a limited background check, coordinated by the classified information security officer, for personnel with access to the protected discovery.

September 11 Damages

The consolidated civil actions against airlines and security companies for damages resulting from the September 11, 2001, terrorist attacks required discovery concerning security procedures. The government decided that the Transportation Security Administration (TSA) should screen discovery for "sensitive security information" (SSI), which is secret information related to transportation security. *In re Sept. 11 Litig.*, 600 F. Supp. 2d 549, 552 (S.D.N.Y. 2009); 49 C.F.R. § 1520.5(a). This slowed substantially the progress of the litigation. *In re Sept. 11 Litig.*, 567 F. Supp. 2d 611, 616 (S.D.N.Y. 2008); *In re Sept. 11 Litig.*, 621 F. Supp. 2d 131, 142 (S.D.N.Y. 2009).

It took the TSA two years to screen an early set of discovery. *In re Sept. 11 Litig.*, 236 F.R.D. 164, 167 (S.D.N.Y. 2006). Then the TSA instructed the defendants to refuse to answer any deposition questions that called for SSI, and the TSA refused to attend the depositions. The district court concluded that the TSA's reasons for intervening in the case required the agency's attendance at the depositions.

The district judge suggested that representative plaintiff attorneys attend the depositions, but many plaintiffs' attorneys were unwilling to be represented by other parties' attorneys. The government, however, wanted to limit the number of people given access to sensitive discovery. Depositions could proceed once the government relaxed its insistence that deposition participation be limited.

Guantánamo Bay

In habeas actions on behalf of Guantánamo Bay detainees, the government sought to keep under seal substantial portions of the case files to protect information that was not classified but was nonetheless considered sensitive. In addition, the detainees' attorneys sometimes sought to protect personal information about their clients that the clients considered sensitive. The court balanced requests to keep parts of the court records sealed against the public's First Amendment and common-law rights.

Giving State Secrets to Lobbyists

In a sting prosecution of lobbyists for sharing classified information, the judge ruled that the indictment required proof that the information passed by the defendants qualified as national defense information (NDI). *United States v. Rosen*, 599 F. Supp. 2d 690, 694–95 (E.D. Va. 2009); *United States v. Rosen*, 471 F. Supp. 2d 651, 652 (E.D. Va. 2007); *see* 18 U.S.C. § 793 (2006). "To qualify as NDI, information must be closely held by the government and potentially damaging to national security if disclosed." *United States v. Rosen*, 487 F. Supp. 2d 703, 705 n.1 (E.D. Va. 2007). "It is important to recognize that NDI and classified material may not be coextensive sets." *Id.* "In short, the government designates what information is labeled and treated as classified, while a court or jury determines what information qualifies as NDI . . . ." *Rosen*, 599 F. Supp. 2d 690.

Filings and Proceedings

If a case involves classified information, then part of the case record may be classified. Security precautions greater than those ordinarily used for sealing part of a record typically are required. Classified information security officers provided by the Justice Department's Litigation Security Group must control classified portions of a case record. They will provide case-specific guidance; the following is only a cursory introduction.

If a party or the court enters into the record a document containing classified information, or a document that might contain classified information, then the document is filed with the classified information security officer instead of with the clerk's office, and the document is deemed filed with the clerk. It is good practice to simultaneously file a public document that gives public notice of the classified filing. The filing of a "half sheet" works well: the part of the first page containing the caption of the case and an unclassified title of the document is placed in the public file. The public record must not include classified information.

Often, unclassified parts of a document containing classified information can be in the public file: after a classification review, the document is redacted to remove the classified information. After a classified document is filed with the classified information security officer, the security officer can refer the document to the appropriate part of the intelligence community for a classification review. If the classification review is conducted on an opinion or an order before the document is served on the parties, then the review is performed by persons walled off from persons working with the government's attorneys in the case. After the classification review, the security officer can place into the public file a redacted version of the document.

The parties, or at least their attorneys, may be cleared to receive unredacted copies of the classified document.

Sometimes, judges simultaneously file a public version of an opinion or order and a more complete version containing classified information with the classified information security officer. It is important to remember how difficult it can be to anticipate what must be redacted from a document in a case concerning classified information. The public docket sheet should reflect both filings. It is important for the court to ensure that this method does not keep from the public record information that is neither classified nor properly sealed on specific findings of a need for sealing.

If a public proceeding might concern classified information, the classified information security officer can attend the proceeding to monitor it and interrupt if anyone appears to be about to say something classified. Often the security officer will be accompanied by someone from the intelligence community. It is important for all participants to know what they can and cannot say in public, so in practice the security officer seldom has to interrupt.

If classified information must be discussed at a proceeding, then all or part of the proceeding may be closed. Proceedings involving classified information are often bifurcated into a closed proceeding, at which classified information can be discussed, and an open proceeding. At the closed portion of the proceeding, only persons cleared to hear the classified information to be discussed can be present. The classified information security officer will advise the court on necessary security precautions and coordinate with the U.S. Marshals Service for physical security. For transcripts of proceedings in which classified information is discussed, the court reporter must have a suitable security clearance. A possibly redacted transcript of closed proceedings can often be released publicly after a classification review.

Documents and transcripts containing classified information must be prepared on approved computer equipment. The classified information security officer will provide an approved laptop computer, which cannot have any network or Internet connection and which must be stored in an approved safe or SCIF.

CASE NOTES

Burma

In an action by the Drug Enforcement Administration's attaché in Burma claiming illegal surveillance, the district court initially sealed the whole record. Later, after a different judge assumed responsibility for the case, the court unsealed the case and ordered a classification review of all previous filings. Documents without classified information were put on the public record, as were redacted versions of documents that contained classified information.

First Prosecution for 1998 Embassy Bombings

The court of appeals approved a district court procedure to resolve a suppression motion in the original prosecution for the 1998 bombings of American embassies in Kenya and Tanzania: the district judge determined the reasonableness of searches in Africa by ex parte examination of classified evidence instead of hearing evidence in an adversary proceeding. *In re Terrorist Bombings of U.S. Embassies in East Africa*, 552 F.3d 157, 159, 165–67, 177 (2d Cir. 2008).

Prosecution of a Guantánamo Bay Detainee for 1998 Embassy Bombings

Concerning the 2010 trial of onetime fugitive Ahmed Khalfan Ghailani for the 1998 bombings of American embassies in Kenya and Tanzania, the judge filed seven opinions containing classified information. Each time, the opinion was filed with the classified information security officer and a cover half-sheet was filed on the public record containing only the case caption and the document title. For most opinions, from one day to two weeks later, a redacted copy of the opinion was filed on the public record. For one opinion concerning discovery, the redacted opinion was filed on the public record approximately two months after the original classified opinion was filed.

Twentieth Hijacker

In the prosecution of Zacarias Moussaoui for terrorism conspiracy, filings that might include classified information were not filed directly with the clerk's office. Defense attorneys, who had security clearances, filed their papers with the classified information security officer, who, by order of the court, arranged for screening by the intelligence community within 48 hours. The government was responsible for classification review of its filings. After classification screening, redacted papers were filed with the clerk's office for inclusion in the public record.

Guantánamo Bay

If there was a chance that a filing by a habeas attorney representing a Guantánamo Bay detainee would contain classified information, which included most filings involving matters more substantive than the dates of proceedings, then the filing would be presented to classified information security officers, at which time it was deemed filed with the court.

Classified materials used by habeas attorneys in court had to be transported to the courtroom by cleared couriers, and the proceedings had to be closed.

Opinions in the Guantánamo Bay habeas cases almost always required a classification review before they could be released publicly. Either the review was performed by persons walled off from representatives of the government in the actions before the opinion was issued simultaneously to the parties in complete form and to the public in redacted form, or the classification review was performed after the opinion was released to the parties and a redacted version was placed on the public record later.

Dirty Bomber

Jose Padilla, who was originally detained on a material witness warrant as part of the grand jury investigation of the September 11, 2001, attacks, was transferred to military detention and designated an enemy combatant for an alleged plan to detonate a dirty bomb. *Padilla ex rel. Newman v. Bush*, 233 F. Supp. 2d 564, 571 (S.D.N.Y. 2002). In response to Padilla's habeas corpus petition, the government submitted both a public redacted declaration describing evidence supporting the designation of Padilla as an enemy combatant and an ex parte, in camera classified unredacted declaration. The only information in the unredacted declaration not in the public declaration was the identity of sources and some circumstantial evidence corroborating facts in the redacted declaration. The judge ruled that it was proper to deny Padilla access to the classified declaration unless Padilla rebutted facts presented in the redacted declaration, in which case the judge would give the government a choice between sharing the unredacted declaration with Padilla or withdrawing it.

Paintball

Ali al-Timimi, the spiritual leader of northern Virginia men who played paintball in preparation for violent jihad, was convicted of soliciting others to wage war against the United States and providing services to the Taliban. The court of appeals remanded the case for an investigation of possibly discoverable surveillance. The trial judge held several postremand proceedings, which were closed because matters discussed touched on classified information. After the proceedings, the transcripts were submitted to the classified information security officer for a classification review. After the classification review, the transcripts became public documents, either in whole or in redacted form.

During some of the proceedings, the defendant was present; he was not authorized to hear classified information, so sometimes participants had to speak cryptically.

Detainee Documents

In an FOIA case concerning extraterritorial detentions of terrorism suspects, the government would not permit the law clerks to see some of the classified information presented to the judge even though the law clerks had security clearances. The judge, nevertheless, was able to review government documents with the law clerks present to make rulings on what had to be produced to the plaintiffs. *See, e.g., ACLU v. Dep't of Defense*, 723 F. Supp. 2d 621, 624 (S.D.N.Y. 2010). The judge examined the documents without showing them to anyone else present, and a court reporter without a security clearance transcribed the proceeding. The judge determined which documents had to be produced, either redacted or unredacted, and did not retain the documents.

Chicago

For the prosecution of Muhammad Abdul Hamid Khalil Salah for helping to provide funds to Hamas—a prosecution that involved a substantial amount of classified evidence relating to Salah's imprisonment in Israel—the judge's opinion denying Salah's motion to suppress a confession in Israel was published in the *Federal Supplement* with 19 redactions because of references to classified information. *United States v. Marzook*, 435 F. Supp. 2d 708 (N.D. Ill. 2006). The parties received unredacted copies, and an unredacted original is stored in the judge's chambers safe.

A motion by the government for secrecy procedures protecting testimony from Israeli agents was supported by a classified affidavit from the FBI's assistant director for counterintelligence—the affidavit was stored in the judge's safe rather than in the clerk's office.

The judge set time limits of seven business days for the government to decide what portions of other documents and transcripts related to classified information could be released to the public. *United States v. Abu Marzook*, 412 F. Supp. 2d 913, 928 (N.D. Ill. 2006).

Giving State Secrets to Lobbyists

The judge presiding over a sting prosecution of lobbyists for sharing classified information held several closed pretrial hearings, each of which required a court reporter with a security clearance because the hearings concerned classified information. The judge denied, however, a government motion to try the defendants in closed proceedings. *United States v. Rosen*, 487 F. Supp. 2d 703 (E.D. Va. 2007).

Some of the orders the judge issued in the case are sealed because they contain classified information. On some occasions, the judge issued a public order stating as much as he could on the public record and a sealed order with additional classified details. *United States v. Rosen*, 520 F. Supp. 2d 802, 814 (E.D. Va. 2007); *United States v. Rosen*, 520 F. Supp. 2d 786, 789, 802 (E.D. Va. 2007). On one occasion, a classified order could subsequently be made public.

Lodi

In the Sacramento prosecution of Hamid Hayat for attending a terrorist training camp, and of his father Umer for lying about it, the government filed a notice that it had potentially discoverable classified evidence. Six sealed ex parte in camera submissions and two sealed ex parte in camera hearings followed. The judge filed rulings and orders under seal if they discussed potentially classified information.

Warrantless Wiretaps

In an action challenging a secret and allegedly illegal surveillance program—the action arising from evidence of surveillance in a top-secret document mistakenly disclosed to an Islamic charity during proceedings to freeze the charity's assets for allegedly funding terrorism—the plaintiffs unsuccessfully opposed a motion by the government to deny them further access to the document. The plaintiffs supported their opposition with a declaration of what they remembered about the document. The plaintiffs filed the declaration under seal, but this afforded insufficient protection for classified information. The clerk's office followed its usual procedures for sealed documents: it opened the sealed envelope, made a copy for the judge, and then resealed it. The government determined that the declaration had the same level of classification as the original document, so it had to be stored with the original document in a locked bag in a SCIF. All classified submissions by the government in this case, until the case was transferred as part of a multidistrict consolidation, were stored in the locked bag when the judge was not examining them.

It was difficult for the plaintiffs in this case to determine whom on the government side they could serve with any papers describing the classified evidentiary document. The government said that the identities of persons with clearance to see such documents was a state secret. The solution to this problem was to have the plaintiffs send classified information to the government on a secure fax line, leaving it up to the government to ensure that only authorized persons received the classified information.

In this and related actions before various judges challenging the surveillance program, the government frequently presented to the court classified briefs and declarations designated for judges' eyes only. Sometimes the judge reviewed the document when it was presented. Sometimes the judge delayed reviewing the document until after a public hearing on the matter so there would be no danger of the judge referring to classified information at the hearing. Another approach was to carefully prepare questions for an oral hearing in advance so as to make sure classified information would not be mentioned. Sometimes the judge deferred decision on whether to examine the classified arguments until there was a showing of need for an in camera, ex parte presentation.

A judge in Chicago decided not to rely on classified submissions in ruling on a motion, but he decided to respond to the submissions in a sealed opinion available only to the government and to judges subsequently reviewing the case. *See Terkel v. AT&T*, 441 F. Supp. 2d 899, 902 (N.D. Ill. 2006).

Atlanta

In a prosecution of two young men in Atlanta for preparing for violent jihad by, among other things, making casing videos of strategic landmarks, filings based on classified information received classification reviews for possible redaction. The court denied as overly broad and excessively burdensome a government request that all filings based on discovery, whether classified or not, be filed under seal.

Fort Dix

In a prosecution for conspiracy to attack Fort Dix, the judge had to rule on the validity of FISA warrants. The judge's opinion on the matter is classified. A redacted opinion was filed publicly after review by intelligence agencies, over 16 months after the original was issued. Redactions appear to conceal which agents of Al-Qaeda were the targets of FISA surveillance resulting in evidence against the defendants.

State-Secrets Privilege

The state-secrets privilege is most likely to arise in a civil action against the government or against a party with whom the government shares interests.

The government cannot be required to divulge state secrets. *See* Robert Timothy Reagan, *Keeping Government Secrets: A Pocket Guide for Judges on the State-Secrets Privilege, the Classified Information Procedures Act, and Court Security Officers* 3–7 (Federal Judicial Center 2007). Designation of information as a state secret requires high-level certification. *United States v. Reynolds*, 345 U.S. 1, 7–8 (1952). Although the executive branch has authority over what constitutes a state secret, the judicial branch has authority over its implications in specific cases.

CASE NOTES

Burma

In an action by the Drug Enforcement Administration's attaché in Burma claiming illegal surveillance, the district court reasoned that because the privilege is a judicial doctrine, the court retains the authority to order secret information disclosed in litigation. *Horn v. Huddle*, 647 F. Supp. 2d 55, 62–63 (D.D.C. 2009), *vacated on other grounds*, 699 F. Supp. 236 (D.D.C. 2010).

Mistaken Rendition

A court of appeals affirmed a district court's dismissal on state-secrets grounds of a tort action alleging that because of mistaken identity the government abducted a German citizen on vacation in Macedonia and imprisoned him in secret for five months. *El-Masri v. United States*, 479 F.3d 296 (4th Cir. 2007).

Warrantless Wiretaps

In an action challenging a secret and allegedly illegal surveillance program—the action arising from evidence of surveillance in a top-secret document mistakenly disclosed to an Islamic charity during proceedings to freeze the charity's assets for allegedly funding terrorism—the court of appeals determined that the document and its contents were state secrets. *Al-Haramain Islamic Found. v. Bush*, 507 F.3d 1190, 1204 (9th Cir. 2007). The three judges on the appellate panel reviewed in camera the document and classified arguments supporting its protection under the state-secrets privilege:

> We take very seriously our obligation to review the documents with a very careful, indeed a skeptical, eye, and not to accept at face value the government's claim or justification of privilege. Simply saying "military secret," "national security" or "terrorist threat" or invoking an ethereal fear that disclosure will threaten our nation is insufficient to support the privilege. Sufficient detail must be—and has been—provided for us to make a meaningful examination.

Id. at 1203.

Torture Flights

A court of appeals affirmed a district court's dismissal on state-secrets grounds of a tort action pertaining to extraordinary rendition, finding that the case could not be litigated without endangering state secrets. *Mohamed v. Jeppesen Dataplan, Inc.*, 614 F.3d 1070 (9th Cir. 2010).

Silent Witness Rule

It is not yet well established, but some courts have employed what is often called a silent witness rule to permit public discussion of classified information. *See United States v. Zettl*, 835 F.2d 1059, 1063 (4th Cir. 1987); *United States v. Rosen*, 520 F. Supp. 2d 786 (E.D. Va. 2007). The classified information, such as the identity of a person or a country, is referred to in code (such as "person 1" or "country A"). The judge, the parties, and the jury know the code but the public does not.

CASE NOTES

September 11 Damages

One action against airlines and security companies for damages resulting from the September 11, 2001, terrorist attacks came close to going to trial, but it ultimately settled. The court prepared for evidence based on "sensitive security information" (SSI), which is protected, but not classified, information related to transportation security. The court issued a protective order calling for use of the silent witness rule at trial.

Giving State Secrets to Lobbyists

For a sting prosecution of lobbyists for sharing classified information, which the government dismissed because of other pretrial rulings, the judge determined that it might be appropriate to introduce classified evidence at trial using the "silent witness rule." *United States v. Rosen*, 520 F. Supp. 2d 786 (E.D. Va. 2007). The silent witness rule permits some evidence to be presented to the judge, the jury, and the parties, but not to the public. It is a partial closing of the trial. The judge determined that the silent witness rule would be appropriate

> only when the government established (i) an overriding reason for closing the trial, (ii) that the closure is no broader than necessary to protect that interest, (iii) that no reasonable alternatives exist to closure, and (iv) that the use of the [silent witness rule] provides defendants with substantially the same ability to make their defense as full public disclosure of the evidence, presented without the use of codes.

Id. at 799.

Special Judicial Resources

As with other cases, in national security cases the court may want to consider both usual and creative ways to manage a case in the interests of justice. For Guantánamo Bay habeas cases, the court used senior judges and magistrate judges for matters common to cases before assigned judges. For a civil challenge to a government program, one judge considered using a special master to advise the court on national security issues.

CASE NOTES

Guantánamo Bay

The district court for the District of Columbia presided over several hundred habeas corpus petitions filed on behalf of Guantánamo Bay detainees. The court referred preliminary matters in the first few cases to a retired senior judge. Another senior judge handled preliminary matters later. A magistrate judge presided over matters concerning habeas attorneys' contacts with their clients.

Warrantless Wiretaps

In an action challenging a secret and allegedly illegal surveillance program, the judge considered naming a court-appointed national security expert "to assist the court in determining whether disclosing particular evidence would create a 'reasonable danger' of harming national security." *Hepting v. AT&T Corp.*, 439 F. Supp. 2d 974, 1010–11 (N.D. Cal. 2006). The government objected to the suggestion, and the judge never decided that such an appointment was necessary.

Courts of Appeals

Appeals are typically heard by three judges with chambers in three different locations, all of which may be different from the place of hearing, and this poses a logistical challenge for the handling of classified information in the appeal.

Classified information may be present in the lower court record, the briefing, and oral argument. If part of the briefing is classified, it is proper for redacted briefs to be filed publicly and unredacted briefs to be filed with the classified information security officer. Some clerk's offices are equipped with storage facilities for classified information, depending on the level of classification. Frequently, classified information security officers or cleared court personnel transport classified briefing between the location of storage and the judge. Sometimes, judges review classified briefing or classified portions of the record while they are at the court to hear other appeals.

Some appellate law clerks obtain security clearances to assist judges with cases concerning classified information. Nevertheless, sometimes the case file includes classified information designated for judges' eyes only.

The membership of an appellate panel and the identity of judges writing opinions are determined well in advance of that information's becoming public, so courts work with the classified information security officers to protect the confidentiality of the judges the security officers are visiting. It is important for judges to be confident that case assignments will not be leaked to government attorneys, for example, in advance of the information's becoming public.

If it is likely that classified information will be discussed at oral argument, part of the argument will be closed. A classified information security officer will attend the open portion to interrupt if it appears that classified information will be disclosed. If the argument is recorded for public broadcast, arrangements are typically made for a delay to ensure that classified information is not inadvertently released publicly.

The court may elect to have its opinion reviewed for redaction of classified information. This review is performed in confidence and shielded from the parts of the government acting as a party in the case. If redaction is necessary, then a redacted opinion will be issued publicly and the unredacted opinion will be provided only to those cleared to see it. Classified information must not appear on the public record, and it is important for courts to keep in mind their limited expertise in what is classified and what is not.

CASE NOTES

Twentieth Hijacker

The court of appeals' clerk's office anticipated that the prosecution of Zacarias Moussaoui for terrorism conspiracy would result in an appeal that included classified information in the court record. So the clerk's office worked with the classified information security officer to (1) create a SCIF and (2) begin the process of obtaining security clearances for several staff members. In 2009, the court worked with the classified information security officer to establish a new SCIF suitable for working in and meeting in, in addition to storage.

Judges can review classified information stored in the court's SCIF in Richmond, Virginia, when they are in town for oral arguments. At judges' home chambers, they can review classified documents stored in SCIFs in one of two ways. Either the classified information security officer can bring classified documents to the judges, or the documents can be stored in nearby SCIFs for the judges to review there. For example, Judge Wilkins had chambers in Greenville, South Carolina, and the courthouse there has a SCIF. Judge Williams had chambers in Orangeburg, South Carolina, which is approximately 50 miles from an FBI SCIF in Columbia. Judge Shedd's Columbia chambers are much nearer to the FBI SCIF in Columbia.

Judge Gregory's home chambers are in Richmond, so he always has ready access to the court of appeals' SCIF. He does not have a career law clerk, and security clearances can take such a large fraction of a temporary law clerk's tenure to acquire that he relies on a court of appeals staff attorney, who has a security clearance, to help him with matters involving classified information.

Briefs containing classified information were filed with the classified information security officer, and redacted briefs were filed in the public record. While the defendant was pro se, he filed many papers with the court of appeals as well as with the district court. The court of appeals typically regarded the filings as appeals, which were reviewed and dismissed. The court worked out a procedure with the jail where the defendant was being detained: the jail would forward a filing directly to the classified information security officer, who would notify the court that a document had been received. After a security review, a redacted version of the document would be filed in the public record.

For an unsuccessful petition to rehear en banc a ruling on an interlocutory discovery appeal, full briefs were filed in the court's Richmond SCIF, and redacted copies were sent to each judge. Some judges opted to review the full briefs in Richmond, and some judges opted to rely on the redacted briefs.

Four appeals were heard in this case, and all oral arguments included both a public session and a closed session at which classified information could be discussed. At the public session, a classified information security officer and a CIA officer attended to monitor the proceeding in case it needed to be interrupted to prevent disclosure of classified information. At these public sessions, no interruption was necessary.

Dirty Bomber

In the habeas corpus appeal of Jose Padilla—originally detained as an alleged dirty bomber but later tried for terrorism conspiracy—the court of appeals reviewed classified declarations presented to the district court but found that it could decide the case without relying on them. *Padilla v. Rumsfeld*, 352 F.3d 695, 701 n.4 (2d Cir. 2003).

A Plot to Kill President Bush

In the appeal of Ahmed Omar Abu Ali, who was convicted of terrorism conspiracy and conspiracy to kill the President, part of the record and part of the briefing were classified. *United States v. Abu Ali*, 528 F.3d 210, 244 n.13 (4th Cir. 2008). Some of the materials were designated for judges' eyes only, which meant that even law clerks with security clearances could not see them. Classified materials were filed through the classified information security officer. Classified materials for this case had to be stored in a SCIF, so judges either viewed them while in Richmond, Virginia, for a session or by using a SCIF near home chambers. Communications among members of the panel about classified matters could happen only in person or by secure fax. Part of oral argument was conducted in closed session.

Mistaken Rendition

The Court of Appeals for the Fourth Circuit affirmed a district court's dismissal, on state-secrets grounds, of a complaint alleging that the CIA abducted and imprisoned Khaled el-Masri until the agency realized that it had picked up the wrong person. *El-Masri v. Tenet*, 479 F.3d 296 (4th Cir. 2007). The three judges hearing the appeal reviewed a classified declaration designated for judges' eyes only while they were in Richmond, Virginia, where the court sits. One judge made a special trip from Charleston, West Virginia, to review the declaration; the other judges reviewed the declaration when they were in town to hear other cases. Deputy clerks with security clearances transported the declaration from the court's SCIF to each judge's chambers, and back again, for the judges' private reviews. While considering el-Masri's unsuccessful petition for certiorari, two Supreme Court justices also reviewed the classified declaration.

Giving State Secrets to Lobbyists

The court of appeals heard expedited appeals of district court rulings on classified evidence in a sting prosecution of lobbyists for sharing classified information. *United States v. Rosen*, 557 F.3d 192, 197 (4th Cir. 2009). Briefing included classified information, so classified briefs were filed with the classified information security officer, and redacted briefs were filed in the public record. Judges reviewed classified briefs either while they were in Richmond to hear an earlier case or at a SCIF near their home chambers. Parts of oral arguments were held in closed sessions so that the parties could discuss classified information with the court. Eight portions of the court of appeals' published opinion resolving the district judge's rulings on classified evidence are redacted.

Warrantless Wiretaps

Judges hearing appeals in actions challenging a secret and allegedly illegal surveillance program by the National Security Agency were asked by the government to receive classified ex parte arguments. Typically, the government lodged complete classified briefs and declarations for in camera review by the judges and filed redacted versions of these documents for the public record. Plaintiffs were not granted access to any classified information in these cases. One proceeding before the Court of Appeals for the Sixth Circuit was conducted under seal with both sides present, but plaintiffs otherwise had access only to public filings and proceedings.

Classified information security officers do not disclose to persons outside the court, including attorneys representing the government, their visits to judges' chambers before the judges assigned to the appeal or the judge assigned to write the opinion has been made public.

The Court of Appeals for the Ninth Circuit permitted C-SPAN to televise oral argument so long as the program was not aired until after the court had an opportunity to excise any inadvertently disclosed secrets, a contingency that did not occur. The classified information security officer offered to review the court's opinion for inadvertently disclosed classified information before the opinion's release, but the court declined the offer.

Torture Flights

For a Ninth Circuit en banc panel review of a district court's dismissal on state-secrets grounds of a tort action pertaining to extraordinary rendition, circuit judges could review classified ex parte briefing and declarations (1) in their chambers, delivered by a classified information security officer, or (2) in San Francisco, while in town for oral arguments.

Classified information security officers received advance notice that the case would be reheard en banc, but they keep such information confidential with respect to units of the government responsible for representing the government as a party.

Putting the Cat Back in the Bag

Occasionally classified information is inadvertently put into the public record or disclosed to someone who should not have received it. This occurrence typically presents a choice between corrective action, which might draw additional attention to the classified information, and a hope that the matter will be minimally noticed.

It is difficult to describe specific instances of this unfortunate occurrence without drawing further attention to classified information.

The court security officer must be consulted in the crafting of a remedy to inadvertently disclosed classified information.

CASE NOTES

Twentieth Hijacker

In the prosecution of Zacarias Moussaoui for terrorism conspiracy, even while the defendant was appearing pro se he was not supposed to have access to classified information. But, the government inadvertently included classified materials among documents produced to him. The government told the district judge that two documents produced to Moussaoui had mistakenly not been marked classified and asked that a "walled-off FBI team" search the defendant's cell to retrieve the documents. The judge determined that even a walled-off FBI team would not adequately protect the defendant's work product. Instead, the judge permitted the U.S. Marshals Service, in consultation with the classified information security officer, to search the prison cell for the two documents plus an additional five that the government identified in the interim as improperly produced. Of the seven searched for, five were found. By the following week, the government presented to the judge a list of 43 improperly produced documents. Many of the documents were prepared by FBI agents who were brought into September 11 investigations without sufficient training in handling and labeling classified information. Eventually, the documents were retrieved and properly marked as classified.

Warrantless Wiretaps

It is important to ensure that information redacted from the public record is redacted effectively. In an action challenging a secret and allegedly illegal surveillance program, a defendant telecommunication company electronically filed a brief with several lines redacted, but the redacted text could be retrieved easily from the electronic document. When this was brought to the court's attention, the electronic text file was replaced with an electronic image file. The redacted information in this case was not classified, but was at most trade secrets.

Part II
Other Issues

Attorney–Client Issues

Attorney–client issues in national security prosecutions are similar to the issues in other criminal cases, but they tend to occur more frequently and be more serious.

Criminal Justice Act Appointments

Acting as a defense attorney in a prosecution for terrorism or espionage often requires special skills and a security clearance. Courts appointing defense counsel in national security cases often have to consider whether to make appointments outside of the routine selection of attorneys pursuant to the Criminal Justice Act.

Sometimes defense attorneys cannot obtain security clearances, and sometimes they are unwilling to submit to the necessary background checks. Courts sometimes appoint a cleared attorney to assist in a defense if only part of the case involves classified information. If the defendant elects to proceed pro se, then courts often appoint cleared counsel as backup.

CASE NOTES

Plot to Bomb New York City Tunnels and Landmarks

El Sayyid Nosair was a coconspirator of the blind sheik Omar Abdel Rahman in a plot to bomb New York City tunnels and landmarks in the 1990s. When the indictment was filed, Nosair was in prison on a state conviction related to the killing of Rabbi Meir Kahane, a former member of the Israeli parliament. *United States v. Rahman*, 189 F.3d 88, 105 & n.3 (2d Cir. 1999). Michael Warren had represented Nosair at the state murder trial. Warren had also appeared on behalf of Ibrahim el-Gabrowny, the first-indicted member of the bombing conspiracy, at el-Gabrowny's first appearance on a criminal complaint filed in advance of the indictment. The district court denied Nosair's request that Warren be appointed under the Criminal Justice Act (CJA), as an exception to regular CJA procedures. Instead, the court appointed a CJA panel attorney.

Prosecution of a Guantánamo Bay Detainee for 1998 Embassy Bombings

Ahmed Khalfan Ghailani was indicted in 1998 for participation in the bombing of the American embassies in Kenya and Tanzania, but after his capture in 2004 he was transferred to Guantánamo Bay until 2009, when he was transferred to the district court. *United States v. Ghailani*, 751 F. Supp. 2d 515, 518 (S.D.N.Y. 2010). Military commission proceedings had been initiated at Guantánamo Bay, and Ghailani asked that his military lawyers continue to represent him. But the Department of Defense did not consent to Ghailani's request, and the district judge ruled that an indigent defendant does not have a constitutional right to select counsel.

The judge did agree to dismiss one appointed attorney because of the defendant's dissatisfaction with him.

Lackawanna

For the high-profile prosecution of six Lackawanna men for attending a violent jihadist training camp in Afghanistan, a magistrate judge made a deliberate effort to appoint well-known and well-respected attorneys, including the federal defender, to represent the defendants.

Fort Dix

After being successfully prosecuted for conspiracy to attack Fort Dix, four defendants sought new counsel for their appeals. The district court determined that circumstances did not justify departure from the usual practice of trial counsel continuing on appeal.

Conflicts of Interest

In criminal cases, conflicts of interest are avoided by codefendants having separate counsel. Because conflicts are waivable, courts must often grapple with attorney and client preferences that could create conflicts.

CASE NOTES

Plot to Bomb New York City Tunnels and Landmarks

The first defendant indicted in the 1990s prosecution for a plot to bomb New York City tunnels and landmarks was Ibrahim el-Gabrowny, who was initially indicted for assaulting federal agents executing a search warrant of his home. *United States v. El-Gabrowny*, 35 F.3d 63, 64 (2d Cir. 1994). After one of the 1993 World Trade Center bombers, Mohammad A. Salameh, failed four attempts to get a New Jersey driver's license, he got a New York driver's license using el-Gabrowny's address, so agents obtained a warrant to search the home as part of the investigation of the World Trade Center bombing. *United States v. Rahman*, 189 F.3d 88, 108 (2d Cir. 1999).

El-Gabrowny was represented by William M. Kunstler, a famous defense lawyer, *see* Albert Ruben, *The People's Lawyer: The Center for Constitutional Rights and the Fight for Social Justice, From Civil Rights to Guantánamo* 91 (2011), at a preindictment bail hearing on a criminal complaint filed the day after the search. *United States v. Rahman*, 837 F. Supp. 64, 65 (S.D.N.Y. 1993). When the indictment was superseded to include Siddig Ibrahim Siddig Ali and others as defendants, Kunstler appeared for both el-Gabrowny and Siddig Ali. Over Kunstler's objection, the district judge appointed for each defendant a CJA panel attorney to advise the defendant of the hazards of joint representation.

Nearly one month after the indictment was expanded to include blind sheik Omar Abdel Rahman, Abdel Rahman's retained attorney notified the court that he could no longer represent his client because they could not agree on a fee agreement. *United States v. Rahman*, 861 F. Supp. 266, 271 (S.D.N.Y. 1994). Kunstler appeared for Abdel Rahman, but the government objected to Kunstler's representing multiple defendants, and the court ruled that Kunstler could represent either el-Gabrowny and Siddig Ali or Abdel Rahman, but not all three. Abdel Rahman opted to represent himself, and the judge appointed a CJA panel attorney to assist him. Abdel Rahman was fully represented by the time of trial.

Seven months before trial, Siddig Ali obtained substitute counsel to help him try to cooperate with the government, but the government decided not to strike a deal. The district court determined that Kunstler could not resume representation of Siddig Ali because of Siddig Ali's actions adverse to the interests of Kunstler's other past and present clients. The court also determined that Kunstler's various current and previous associations with several defendants in the case meant that he could no longer represent el-Gabrowny.

First Prosecution for 1998 Embassy Bombings

A severe conflict of interest arose when a defendant in the prosecution for the 1998 bombings of American embassies in Kenya and Tanzania stabbed a prison guard, because the defendant's attorneys were not only witnesses to the stabbing but potential targets of a more elaborate scheme of violence. *United States v. Bin Laden*, 160 F. Supp. 2d 670, 673 (S.D.N.Y. 2001). Because the trial was scheduled to begin only two months later, the defendant was severed from the trial. He pleaded guilty to attempted murder for the stabbing and has not been tried for the bombings.

Prosecution of a Charity

In the prosecution of the Holy Land Foundation and all of its principals for providing funds to Hamas, the foundation and its CEO were represented by the same attorney until the eve of trial on a waiver of conflict signed by the foundation's chairman. At the pretrial oral conflict colloquy, the attorney for the chairman announced that he was not sure his client could speak for the foundation. The attorney for the CEO said that she was not sure anyone could speak for the foundation, so the judge allowed her to withdraw as the foundation's attorney, and the trial proceeded without the foundation's having representation. A mistrial resulted from the jury's deadlock on counts against all defendants, and a different judge presided over the retrial because of the first judge's taking senior status and no longer taking criminal cases. Because the docket sheet did not reflect the foundation's attorney's withdrawal, the second judge did not know that the foundation was not represented until sentencing. The sentencing judge determined that the foundation had de facto representation because of its common interests with the other defendants, and the issue is now on appeal.

Atlanta

In a prosecution of two young men in Atlanta for preparing for violent jihad by, among other things, making casing videos of strategic landmarks, Ehsanul Islam Sadequee was represented by the federal defender's office. Sadequee was assaulted in detention by another inmate who was also represented by that office. The office, therefore, could no longer represent Sadequee, and another attorney was appointed.

Communication

Communication between defense attorneys and their clients in national security cases can be made complicated by (1) the attorneys' not being able to share classified information with their clients and (2) security measures that infringe on the privacy or even possibility of attorney–client communications.

CASE NOTES

First Prosecution for 1998 Embassy Bombings

When the original defendants in the prosecution for the 1998 bombings of American embassies in Kenya and Tanzania were detained, they were cut off from virtually all communications. *United States v. Bin Laden*, 92 F. Supp. 2d 225, 231–32 (S.D.N.Y. 2000). The defendants were permitted to meet with their attorneys, but the attorneys were prohibited from sharing anything said in the attorney–defendant meetings with investigators or experts, which seriously hampered the preparation of a defense.

Millennium Bomber

Because of an error by personnel at a Canadian courthouse, the attorneys representing Ahmed Ressam, who planned to drive from Canada to bomb the Los Angeles International Airport at the turn of the millennium, were permitted to copy certain documents in Canada, but they had to surrender the copies when the error was discovered. The U.S. prosecution moved for an order prohibiting the attorneys from discussing the documents with their client. The district judge told the attorneys that they could use the information that they obtained from the Canadian files as a last resort, but they could not disclose to their client the origin of the information.

Guantánamo Bay

Information provided to their habeas attorneys by Guantánamo Bay detainees was presumptively classified. A "privilege review team," walled off from attorneys representing the government in litigation, performed a classification review on detainee communications and their lawyers' notes.

Dirty Bomber

Jose Padilla, who was originally detained on a material witness warrant as part of the grand jury investigation of the September 11, 2001, attacks, was transferred to military detention and designated an enemy combatant for an alleged plan to detonate a dirty bomb. *Padilla ex rel. Newman v. Bush*, 233 F. Supp. 2d 564, 571 (S.D.N.Y. 2002). The government denied Padilla access to counsel upon his transfer to military custody, arguing that Padilla might use contacts with counsel to communicate with other terrorists. The district court determined that Padilla was entitled to counsel "for purposes of presenting facts to the court in connection with" a habeas corpus petition.

Paintball

In the prosecution of Ali al-Timimi, the spiritual leader of northern Virginia men who played paintball in preparation for violent jihad, defense attorneys claimed that the Bureau of Prisons opened the defendant's clearly labeled attorney–client mail and transferred the defendant so frequently from prison to prison that it was difficult for the attorneys to know where he was and make arrangements to see him. The judge ordered the defendant returned to the district.

Toledo

In a prosecution of Americans for conspiracy to fight against U.S. forces in Iraq, defense attorneys became concerned that their communications with their clients were being improperly monitored. Defense attorneys filed a motion to compel the government to describe with particularity how their clients' communications were monitored, and government attorneys responded that they were not aware of any monitoring beyond the ordinary.

Rapport

Terrorism defendants' attitudes toward the U.S. system of justice often range from distrust to hatred. This often makes rapport between defendants and their attorneys, especially appointed attorneys, difficult.

When appointing an attorney to represent a terrorism defendant, the court may want to consider the attorney's experience with difficult clients or with clients from other cultures. There are many potential pitfalls. For example, attorneys often use humor to foster rapport with their clients, but that strategy is frequently risky in these cases.

Terrorism defendants may be more likely than other criminal defendants to act against the advice of counsel, such as by pleading guilty or electing to proceed pro se.

CASE NOTES

First Prosecution for 1998 Embassy Bombings

One of the attorneys appointed to represent a defendant in the original prosecution for the 1998 bombings of American embassies in Kenya and Tanzania had to be dismissed for mocking his client's religious beliefs. When the client explained to the attorney his belief that a martyr would have 13 virgin brides in paradise, the attorney jokingly lamented having 13 fathers-in-law. On the next morning, the judge found on his desk a request by the defendant for a new attorney. The judge granted the request.

Defendant Mamdouth Mahmud Salim stabbed a prison guard two months in advance of his scheduled trial. *In re Terrorist Bombings of U.S. Embassies in East Africa*, 552 F.3d 93, 150 (2d Cir. 2008); *United States v. Salim*, 549 F.3d 67, 70 (2d Cir. 2008). Salim's attorneys may have been targets of a more elaborate scheme of violence. *United States v. Salim*, 287 F. Supp. 2d 250, 250 (S.D.N.Y. 2003). The district judge observed, "Lawyers don't often represent somebody who hates them, who, all things being considered, would just as soon kill them. How you maintain an attorney–client relationship under those circumstances is very difficult." *Trying Cases Related to Allegations of Terrorism: Judges' Roundtable*, 77 Fordham L. Rev. 1, 13 (2008).

Twentieth Hijacker

The district court appointed the federal defender and a private attorney to represent Zacarias Moussaoui in his prosecution for terrorism conspiracy. *United States v. Moussaoui*, 591 F.3d 263, 267 (4th Cir. 2010). The defendant had a strained relationship with his attorneys, especially with the private attorney. At a hearing on conditions of confinement, four months after his indictment, Zacarias Moussaoui announced that he would like to represent himself, possibly with the assistance of a Muslim attorney, because his assigned attorneys did not understand Muslims. *Id.* at 269–70; *United States v. Moussaoui*, 333 F.3d 509, 512–13 (4th Cir. 2003).

Moussaoui identified a Muslim attorney in Texas whom he wanted to consult with, but this attorney never made an appearance, never sought admission to the court's bar, and never consented to the screening required for the security clearance that would be needed to represent Moussaoui in court.

While Moussaoui was proceeding pro se, the district judge appointed a second private attorney as standby counsel; by the end of the case, this was the attorney that the defendant was most willing to talk to because the defendant judged him to be the most respectful.

Toledo
In a prosecution of Americans for conspiracy to fight against U.S. forces in Iraq, the judge appointed the federal defender's office as counsel for one of the defendants. The defendant was concerned that a government employee would not represent him adequately, and the judge reluctantly agreed to appoint substitute counsel. The defendant, however, was no more satisfied with substitute counsel, and he eventually asked the judge to reappoint the federal defender's office, which the judge did.

Conditions of Detention

Conditions of detention for persons accused of doing harm to our national security are often very strict. Strict detention security measures are sometimes referred to as special administrative measures (SAMs).

Judges are often attentive to the possibility that security measures will impair an effective defense, especially with respect to the confidentiality and effectiveness of attorney–client communications and the defendant's mental health.

Security

Security measures for national security defendants can include solitary confinement. Security is tight to prevent defendants from communicating with conspirators. Also, national security defendants are often at an elevated risk of harm from other inmates.

Courts have not found incarceration necessary to ensure all national security defendants' presence for trial. Bail, perhaps with electronic monitoring or home detention, has been found sufficient for some.

CASE NOTES

First Prosecution for 1998 Embassy Bombings
When the original defendants in the prosecution for the 1998 bombings of American embassies in Kenya and Tanzania were detained, they were held in solitary confinement. *United States v. Bin Laden*, 92 F. Supp. 2d 225, 231–32 (S.D.N.Y. 2000). In response to complaints by defense attorneys, the district judge visited the jail and approved the conditions of detention, except that he ordered that the defendants be permitted to call their families three times a month instead of once. *United States v. El-Hage*, 213 F.3d 74, 77 (2d Cir. 2000).

Minneapolis
Mohamed Abdullah Warsame, who was indicted for attending Al-Qaeda training camps, was held in solitary pretrial detention for over five years. The district judge observed a resulting decline in the defendant's mental health. The case was resolved by a plea bargain.

Chicago
In the prosecution of Muhammad Abdul Hamid Khalil Salah and Abdelhaleem Hasan Abdelraziq for helping to provide funds to Hamas, the judge permitted friends and relatives to post nearly $4 million worth of property to secure detention by home confinement.

Toledo

In a prosecution of Americans for conspiracy to fight against U.S. forces in Iraq, the judge decided that one of the defendants could be released on bond with electronic monitoring.

Access to Counsel

Because the government is worried about terrorism suspects' communicating with terrorism conspirators, either directly or indirectly, there is often an effort to restrict or monitor counsel visits with and communication with their clients. Judges frequently attend to the possibility of excessive restrictions or monitoring. Sometimes judges intervene formally. Sometimes more informal inquiries and suggestions can achieve positive results.

CASE NOTES

Dirty Bomber

In the trial of Jose Padilla—who was originally detained as a dirty bomber but ultimately tried with two other men for terrorism conspiracy—the district court was called upon to issue orders directing the detention center to provide defendants with adequate access to counsel. One order granted defendants two 15-minute telephone calls with their attorneys each week: "During these legal telephone calls the [federal detention center] officials shall stay a reasonable distance away from the Defendant to allow for sufficient privacy." Order, *United States v. Hassoun*, No. 0:04-cr-60001 (S.D. Fla. Sept. 21, 2005). As trial approached, the judge ordered the detention center to provide a larger conference table for meetings between the defendants and their attorneys.

Minneapolis

Mohamed Abdullah Warsame, who was indicted for attending Al-Qaeda training camps, was represented by the federal defender's office. For a time, the government imposed restrictions on who in the defender's office could communicate with Warsame, and the defender's office could not agree to the restrictions. Eventually, the two sides were able to work out an agreement.

Mental Health

Strict conditions of detention, especially solitary confinement, can have a negative impact on a defendant's mental health. Judges often attend to this possibility to ensure that the defendant's ability to participate in his defense is not impaired.

Courts must nevertheless be wary of false or exaggerated claims of mental health impairment.

For a defendant held in solitary confinement as a preventive security measure, court appearances can be therapeutic. On the other hand, sometimes body searches performed on defendants as they are transported between court and the place of confinement can be unpleasant.

CASE NOTES

First Prosecution for 1998 Embassy Bombings

During a hearing, after several months of restrictive confinement, Wadih el-Hage, one of the defendants in the prosecution for the 1998 bombings of American embassies in Africa, angrily criticized the district judge for not reading a letter el-Hage had prepared proclaiming his innocence and contending that the United States could have prevented the bombings. *In re Terrorist Bombings of U.S. Embassies in East Africa*, 552 F.3d 93, 149 (2d Cir. 2008). Deputy marshals restrained the defendant when he leapt from his chair in the courtroom and appeared to charge the judge. Approximately six months later, a psychiatrist reported that el-Hage's solitary confinement was seriously impairing his mental health. The prison agreed to give el-Hage a cell mate, but the court ruled that his conditions of confinement were largely proper, and el-Hage complained that the cell mate made his cell too crowded.

After a prison guard was stabbed by a codefendant, an incident not involving el-Hage, the prison removed el-Hage's possessions and privileges. According to his wife, his mental state deteriorated sharply and he stopped recognizing his attorney. However, two court-appointed psychiatrists and a court-appointed psychologist determined that el-Hage was faking mental illness. The judge decided that the expert opinions were well founded and that el-Hage was competent to stand trial.

Prosecution of a Guantánamo Bay Detainee for 1998 Embassy Bombings

During the 2010 prosecution of Ahmed Khalfan Ghailani, a onetime fugitive, for the 1998 bombings of American embassies in Kenya and Tanzania, the defendant complained that intrusive body cavity searches every time he appeared in court were causing him post-traumatic stress disorder. The district judge determined that the defendant was not suffering from post-traumatic stress disorder and denied relief. *United States v. Ghailani*, 751 F. Supp. 2d 508, 514 (S.D.N.Y. 2010). The defendant began to appear in court less frequently.

Guantánamo Bay

Guantánamo Bay detainees occasionally protested their confinement with hunger strikes and, more rarely, suicide attempts, some of which were successful. The district court determined that Congress had stripped the detainees of habeas rights concerning the conditions of their confinement, but that they could challenge conditions that affected their abilities to work with their attorneys on their cases, so the court sometimes was called on to issue orders concerning detainees' medical issues.

Dirty Bomber

Jose Padilla, who was originally detained on a material witness warrant as part of the grand jury investigation of the September 11, 2001, attacks, was transferred to military detention and designated an enemy combatant for an alleged plan to detonate a dirty bomb. *Padilla ex rel. Newman v. Bush*, 233 F. Supp. 2d 564, 571 (S.D.N.Y. 2002). During his military detention, the government applied substantial psychological pressure as part of the detainee's interrogation. *Padilla ex rel. Newman v. Rumsfeld*, 243 F. Supp. 2d 42, 43 (S.D.N.Y. 2003). Padilla was subsequently transferred to civilian custody for a trial with two other men for terrorism conspiracy, unrelated to a dirty bomb, and Padilla's attorneys claimed that the psychological pressure during military detention had resulted in incapacitating post-traumatic stress disorder. Because the security measures imposed for Padilla's pretrial detention made psychiatric evaluation difficult within the detention center, the district judge provided her courtroom, without the judge present, for the evaluation. The judge found Padilla competent to stand trial.

For security reasons, Padilla and his codefendants were detained in solitary confinement. Three months after they were convicted, one defendant attempted suicide.

Minneapolis

Mohamed Abdullah Warsame, who was indicted for attending Al-Qaeda training camps, was held in solitary pretrial detention for over five years. For the sake of the defendant's mental health, the judge encouraged the defendant's attendance at proceedings, which afforded him time outside his cell and time in the presence of other people. Warsame was a Canadian citizen, and visits by the Canadian consulate were also helpful.

Cultural Accommodation

Prosecutions for assaults on national security may entail elements of cultural diversity. Judges strive to prevent cultural differences from creating distractions from the pursuit of justice.

For example, prosecutions of Muslim defendants as suspected terrorists have accommodated breaks for prayers and religious holidays. Some judges take testimony by affirmation rather than by oath so that jurors are not biased by unnecessary religious references.

CASE NOTES

First Prosecution for 1998 Embassy Bombings

The district judge carefully timed breaks in the trial to permit prayer at the appropriate times by the Muslim defendants, whose entry to and exit from the courtroom were made cumbersome by their hidden shackles.

Twentieth Hijacker

In his prosecution for terrorism conspiracy, Zacarias Moussaoui refused to honor the judge by standing when she entered or left the courtroom, so the judge arranged proceedings so that she and the defendant would enter and leave the courtroom at the same time.

Lackawanna

For the prosecution of six Lackawanna Muslim men for attending a violent jihadist training camp in Afghanistan, the district court timed hearings to accommodate both daily prayers and religious holidays. All testimony at the detention hearing before a magistrate judge was taken from government witnesses under oath, but the defendants' pleas before the district judge were taken by affirmation.

Paintball

In the prosecution of northern Virginia men for playing paintball in preparation for violent jihad and for attending terrorist training camps in the Middle East, the district judge took all testimony by affirmation rather than by oath, a practice she developed so that no bias could result from whether a witness swore on a Bible or a Quran.

Atlanta

In a prosecution of two young men in Atlanta for preparing for violent jihad by, among other things, making casing videos of strategic landmarks, the court appointed a Muslim attorney from a nearby district to represent one of the defendants.

High Profile

National security cases are often high in profile. Sealing parts of the case record and closing some proceedings to protect national security often fosters curiosity in the news media about what they are missing. Otherwise, issues relating to some high-profile national security cases are largely similar to issues that arise in other high-profile cases.

Gag Orders

In high-profile cases, especially criminal cases, judges often consider issuing gag orders restricting the participants' public comments on the cases so that prospective jurors will not be improperly influenced. The parties often stipulate to such orders. Appellate courts work to ensure that gag orders are no more restrictive than necessary.

CASE NOTES

First World Trade Center Bombing

In the prosecution for the 1993 bombing of the World Trade Center, the Court of Appeals for the Second Circuit vacated as overbroad a district court gag order prohibiting attorneys from making any public statements related to the case. *United States v. Salameh*, 992 F.2d 445, 447 (2d Cir. 1993). The district judge issued the gag order orally and sua sponte at arraignments one day after a superseding indictment was filed, which was two weeks after the original indictment was filed. The judge said that his primary interest was retaining venue. But the court of appeals held that the gag order was not narrowly tailored.

> An order that prohibits the utterance or publication of particular information or commentary imposes a "prior restraint" on speech. A prior restraint on constitutionally protected expression, even one that is intended to protect a defendant's Sixth Amendment right to trial before an impartial jury, normally carries a heavy presumption against its constitutional validity.

Id. at 446–47.

Detroit

In the first post-September 11, 2001, prosecution for terrorism, the judge issued a stipulated gag order forbidding public comments about the case that would have a reasonable likelihood of interfering with a fair trial. Eight days later, the Attorney General incorrectly stated at a press conference that the defendants were "suspected of having knowledge of the September 11th attacks." *United States v. Koubriti*, 305 F. Supp. 2d 723, 725, 728–30, 733 (E.D. Mich. 2003). Also, during the trial, the Attorney General commented favorably at a press conference on the credibility of a cooperating codefendant's testimony. The judge issued "a public and formal judicial admonishment of the Attorney General." *Id.* at 726.

Media Attention

Enhanced media attention in a case poses two types of challenge for the court: (1) an increase in the number of people visiting the courthouse, many of whom come with extensive collections of electronic equipment, and (2) an increased expectation of the amount of information provided.

Most news media pay attention only to major events in a case, although some news media may follow the case in greater detail. It is not always predictable what will draw heavy media attention.

Managing the logistics of media attention can be quite a challenge. An increase in the number of persons visiting the courthouse often requires additional security considerations, including attention to the efficiency of security in light of the increased number of visitors. Courts have to address the issue of what electronic equipment can be brought into the courthouse. Even if electronic equipment is forbidden in the courtroom, courts often accommodate it elsewhere in the courthouse, such as in an overflow courtroom.

Logistical issues pertaining to an increase in courthouse visitors often extend to the neighborhood. Courts often work with local authorities to anticipate and manage increased traffic near the courthouse. This increased traffic often includes large media vehicles parked to transmit information.

Media reports on the courthouse steps are a common practice. Because of weather, security, or logistical issues, courts may prefer that media reports be delivered from another location. Courts sometimes have space they can use as a media room for this purpose.

It is helpful to both the court and the media for the court to provide the media with a designated contact person for information and for what the media can expect in terms of schedules, filings, and proceedings. *E.g.*, Steve Leben, *Ten Tips for Judges Dealing with the Media*, 47 Ct. Rev. 38 (2011).

CASE NOTES

Lackawanna

The prosecution of six Lackawanna men for attending a violent jihadist training camp in Afghanistan drew media attention from all over the world. The pretrial detention hearing was held soon after the first anniversary of the September 11, 2001, attacks. The public square in front of the courthouse was filled with large media vans, and there were public picketers in the square and around the courthouse. A popular picket read, "Jail, No Bail." The magistrate judge who conducted the hearing strove to provide the government and the defendants with a fair and peaceful hearing, mindful that the world was watching how the criminal defendants were treated.

Atlanta

A prosecution of two men for preparing for violent jihad by, among other things, making casing videos of strategic landmarks received extensive media coverage, especially by local news media. One local journalist sat through the entire trial.

Several news media attended a routine status conference held in the magistrate judge's chambers, because there had been talk of closing the proceeding. The judge observed that sealing documents and closing proceedings often intensifies news media interest.

Fort Dix

A prosecution for conspiracy to attack Fort Dix received substantial media attention. In part because of the cold December weather in Camden, New Jersey, where the trial was held, the judge did not want press conferences on the steps of the courthouse following the verdict, so news media were asked to gather in the jury assembly room. The government addressed the media for the first half hour; then defense counsel and families of the defendants addressed the media. The media could bring in cameras and recording devices during these presentations. Because it worked well, a similar procedure was used after sentencing.

Reserved Seating

If spectator space in the courtroom will be at a premium, courts often work with the deputy marshals and security officers to ensure that some seating is reserved for the defendants' families, persons affiliated with alleged victims, news media, and the public, respectively.

CASE NOTES

Prosecution of a Guantánamo Bay Detainee for 1998 Embassy Bombings

In the 2010 trial of Ahmed Khalfan Ghailani, a onetime fugitive, for the 1998 bombings of American embassies in Kenya and Tanzania, the judge reserved some seats in the courtroom for the news media.

Atlanta

At a trial of two young men for preparing for violent jihad by, among other things, making casing videos of strategic landmarks, the judge reserved a row of seats for the news media. Because it was a bench trial, the judge permitted sketch artists to sit in the jury box.

Remote Viewing

It is common for courts to set aside at least one additional courtroom during high-profile cases. Proceedings in the main courtroom are displayed in the overflow courtroom audiovisually. In some cases, courts have transmitted proceedings audiovisually to remote locations, such as other courthouses in the district or courthouses in other locations where interest is likely to be high.

Some judges provide the media with an overflow courtroom in which media members can use electronic equipment. On occasion, the news media have been permitted to use some electronic equipment in the main courtroom.

The extent to which overflow courtrooms are actually used, especially in remote locations, is often unpredictable.

CASE NOTES

Twentieth Hijacker

In the penalty trial for Zacarias Moussaoui, to determine whether he should be executed, proceedings were broadcast to viewing sites in Manhattan, Central Islip, Boston, Philadelphia, Newark, and a second courtroom in Alexandria, Virginia, for family members of September 11, 2001, victims. Fewer people watched the proceedings at off-site locations than was anticipated.

Fort Dix

For a high-profile prosecution charging conspiracy to attack Fort Dix, the court designated two overflow courtrooms: one for the news media and one for the rest of the public. Because the judge permitted the media to use laptop computers in the main courtroom and gave them wireless Internet access, they did not use their overflow courtroom. Journalists used the court's wireless Internet access to blog about the case in real time. Recording devices were not permitted in the courtroom, published likenesses of the jurors were prohibited, and members of the public were forbidden from bringing in electronic equipment. The overflow courtroom was needed for the rest of the public on the first day of the trial and on the day of the verdict.

Courtroom Displays of Support or Opposition

Judges typically do not allow persons attending a trial in support of one of the parties to in any sense become a cheering section, especially if the case is tried before a jury.

CASE NOTES

First Prosecution for 1998 Embassy Bombings

In the original trial for the 1998 bombings of American embassies, many survivors of the bombings attended the trial wearing lapel pins, provided by a victims' advocate, showing a map of Africa with Kenya and Tanzania highlighted. The pins helped the deputy marshals identify victims for appropriate seating; but after defense counsel argued that the pins would improperly influence the jurors, the judge ordered that they not be worn.

Making Filings and Evidence Available to News Media

Court filings are now available on the Internet through PACER (Public Access to Court Electronic Records). Use of PACER, however, requires a PACER account. Although filings by the judge typically are available in PACER without charge, other filings are only available for a per-page fee. In a high-profile case, a court will often set up a special webpage at the court's Internet site and post all filings for the case there. That makes these filings available free of charge to anyone with access to the Internet, including news media, without their need to contact the court.

Some courts also work to promptly post on the Internet trial exhibits and even proceeding transcripts.

CASE NOTES

Atlanta

In a prosecution for preparing for violent jihad by, among other things, making casing videos of strategic landmarks, news media had access to all of the evidence on the day that it was admitted. The U.S. Attorney's Office was responsible for providing copies of evidence to the media.

Fort Dix

For a high-profile prosecution charging conspiracy to attack Fort Dix, the court set up a public website where documents in the case file were posted. This allowed access to the documents without going through PACER. Evidence was posted the moment it was admitted. Each side loaded digitized exhibits on a secure server in advance of moving for their admissibility. Neither side had access to the other side's exhibits on the server until they were admitted.

The court also posted proceeding transcripts on the server in a way that permitted free access to the proceedings while protecting the court reporters' proprietary rights in the transcripts. Transcript text rolled on the public website in continuous loops so that a website visitor would see whatever few lines of text were displayed at that moment, and lines of text scrolled by as the viewer looked at the transcript.

Courthouse Security

Concerns about physical security during trials and other proceedings are often heightened in high-profile cases involving persons possibly prone to dangerous behavior or in cases that might attract the interest of persons prone to dangerous behavior.

Sometimes, defendants are discreetly shackled. Sometimes, courts establish additional security at entrances to both the courthouse and the courtroom. The anticipated volume and type of traffic near the courthouse may be a reason for additional perimeter security.

One downside of tight security in a criminal jury trial is a possibly prejudicial message it might send to the jury that the defendants might be dangerous.

CASE NOTES

Plot to Bomb U.S. Airplanes in Southeast Asia

In the trial for conspiracy to bomb American airplanes in southeast Asia, the district judge had to dismiss the first 75 prospective jurors because they indicated that they would be influenced by heavy court security.

First Prosecution for 1998 Embassy Bombings

In the original prosecution for the 1998 bombings of American embassies in Kenya and Tanzania, defendants were always shackled when in the courtroom because of an incident during a hearing in which a defendant began to angrily charge toward the judge. When the jury trial began, a screen at the defense table covered the defendants' shackles and jurors were not present when the defendants were brought in and out. Persons in the courtroom were not asked to rise when the judge entered.

Persons entering the courtroom had to pass through a metal detector and sign a log book stating their purpose in attending the trial. The jury room was guarded by deputy marshals and checked each morning by bomb-sniffing dogs.

The defendants were sentenced on October 18, 2001. *In re Terrorist Bombings of U.S. Embassies in East Africa*, 552 F.3d 93, 102 (2d Cir. 2008); *United States v. Bin Laden*, 397 F. Supp. 2d 465, 474 (S.D.N.Y. 2005). Because of the recent and nearby attacks on September 11, court security on the day of sentencing was substantially enhanced. According to the *New York Times*, "The building resembled a military base, with federal marshals carrying shotguns, public entrances closed and the screening of visitors increased." Benjamin Weiser, *4 Are Sentenced to Life in Prison in 1998 U.S. Embassy Bombings*, N.Y. Times, Oct. 19, 2001, at A1.

Millennium Bomber

At the first appearance in court in Seattle of Ahmed Ressam, who planned to bomb the Los Angeles International Airport at the turn of the millennium, "Security was so tight at the courthouse that anyone entering—even employees—had to produce a photo identification. A phalanx of U.S. marshals also blocked the door to [the magistrate judge's] courtroom and armed officers patrolled the streets as Ressam was brought to the courthouse." Scott Sunde & Elaine Porterfield, *Wider Bomb Plot Possible*, Seattle Post-Intelligencer, Dec. 18, 1999, at A1.

For the subsequent trial in Los Angeles also, security was enhanced, including added patrols, bomb-sniffing dogs, and inspections of cars entering the underground garage.

Twentieth Hijacker

The federal courthouse in Alexandria, Virginia, had never seen such a level of security as it saw for the prosecution of Zacarias Moussaoui for terrorism conspiracy. At his arraignment, Moussaoui arrived before 6:00 a.m., while it was still dark. Deputy marshals surrounded the courthouse, and extra metal detectors were stationed at the courtroom. Although the outside air was frigid, members of the news media and the public were not allowed into the building until shortly before the hearing. At subsequent appearances also, extra deputy marshals guarded the courthouse.

Dirty Bomber

In the Miami trial of three men—including Jose Padilla, who was originally detained as a dirty bomber but was ultimately tried for terrorism conspiracy—federal deputy marshals were brought in from around the country to provide the courthouse with extra security. An extra metal detector was installed outside the courtroom door.

Lackawanna

For the prosecution of six Lackawanna men for attending a violent jihadist training camp in Afghanistan, the marshal established extra security at the courthouse doors. The courthouse received security sweeps three times a day, and security included a bomb-sniffing dog. The defendants pleaded guilty; during the days of pleas and sentences, armed surveillance officers were posted at the windows in the judge's chambers.

Toledo

In a prosecution of Americans for conspiracy to fight against U.S. forces in Iraq, the judge was concerned about the impact on potential jurors of highly visible extra security. For example, parked outside the courthouse was a conspicuously marked Department of Homeland Security SUV. It did not help that one news station reported on the case with a graphic titled, "Terror in Toledo." The judge worked with security forces to convey less of a siege image.

Fort Dix

In a high-profile trial for conspiracy to attack Fort Dix, court security was enhanced. Additional precautions were taken during the two days of sentencing. No other judge scheduled proceedings for those days, and court staff were encouraged to work at home. Because a jury was not present, there was a greater visible presence of security.

Jury Issues

Jury trials in national security cases present issues common to jury trials in other high-profile trials in which security is a matter of concern.

Size of Venire

Sometimes national security trials are long and complex, which means the court will have to assemble a large venire to allow for hardship excuses. Often it is anticipated that the facts of the case will stimulate prejudicial emotions among potential jurors, so judges sometimes allow for extra challenges and a larger venire to accommodate them. On the other hand, sometimes a normal-sized venire can be used for a national security case.

CASE NOTES

First World Trade Center Bombing
According to news media, the district court issued 5,000 extra jury summonses to assemble a jury pool for the trial against those accused of bombing the World Trade Center in 1993.

First Prosecution for 1998 Embassy Bombings
In the original prosecution for the 1998 bombings of American embassies in Kenya and Tanzania, the district judge screened a jury pool of 1,302 people with the help of a questionnaire.

Millennium Bomber
In the prosecution of Ahmed Ressam, who planned to bomb the Los Angeles International Airport at the turn of the millennium, a jury was selected from 44 prospective jurors after a little more than seven hours of voir dire.

Detroit
In the first post-September 11, 2001, prosecution for terrorism, the district court selected 280 prospective jurors for the case.

Twentieth Hijacker
In the prosecution of Zacarias Moussaoui for terrorism conspiracy, the district court sent out more than 1,000 jury summonses and had more than 500 potential jurors fill out jury questionnaires.

Dirty Bomber
In the trial of Jose Padilla, originally detained as a dirty bomber but ultimately tried for terrorism conspiracy, the district judge decided to send out 3,000 jury duty letters for the trial. Jurors were selected from an initial pool of approximately 300, and then from a pool culled using a jury questionnaire of 88 potential jurors.

Anonymous Jury

If defendants are likely to be dangerous or associated with dangerous people, judges often consider using anonymous juries to protect the jurors' safety. Sometimes judges use anonymous juries to protect jurors from media harassment in high-profile cases. Judges are often cautious about using an anonymous jury to protect the jurors' safety, because a suggestion that the jurors are in danger may have a prejudicial impact. On the other hand, jurors' safety is a crucial consideration.

Sometimes the identities of anonymous jurors are known to the judge and the parties, but not the news media or the public; sometimes the jurors' identities are known only to a few members of the clerk of court's staff.

Voir dire of prospective anonymous jurors has sometimes been conducted in closed session. Judges have sometimes accommodated a public right of access to voir dire by releasing redacted transcripts or allowing select news media representatives to attend.

CASE NOTES

First World Trade Center Bombing
The district judge used anonymous juries for the two trials. When an alternate juror's anonymity became at risk in the second trial, the judge dismissed the juror.

Plot to Bomb New York City Tunnels and Landmarks
The district judge used an anonymous jury. Voir dire was conducted in a conference room with the news media represented by two re-

porters—one from print and one from electronic media.

First Prosecution for 1998 Embassy Bombings

In the original trial for the 1998 bombings of American embassies in Kenya and Tanzania, the district judge used an anonymous jury and closed jury selection.

Prosecution of a Guantánamo Bay Detainee for 1998 Embassy Bombings

In the 2010 trial of onetime fugitive Ahmed Khalfan Ghailani, the district judge used an anonymous jury.

Millennium Bomber

In the prosecution of Ahmed Ressam, who planned to bomb the Los Angeles International Airport at the turn of the millennium, the judge was not asked to use an anonymous jury; he has never used one.

Detroit

In the first post-September 11, 2001, prosecution for terrorism, the judge used an anonymous jury and selected the jury behind closed doors. *United States v. Koubriti*, 305 F. Supp. 2d 723, 728 (E.D. Mich. 2003); *United States v. Koubriti*, 252 F. Supp. 2d 424, 426 (E.D. Mich. 2003); *United States v. Koubriti*, 252 F. Supp. 2d 418 (E.D. Mich. 2002) (denying a motion opposing the empanelling of an anonymous jury). After the trial was over, the judge released a redacted transcript of the selection process.

Twentieth Hijacker

In the prosecution of Zacarias Moussaoui for terrorism conspiracy, the district judge used an anonymous jury. Jurors assembled in a secret location and were driven to the courthouse. The court set up a special lunch room for the jurors, away from the public. Jurors were never permitted to be in the building unsupervised.

Dirty Bomber

In the Miami trial of three men—including Jose Padilla, who was originally detained as a dirty bomber but was ultimately tried for terrorism conspiracy—jurors' identities were known to the court and the parties, but identifying information was not presented in open court or otherwise made public.

Chicago

In the prosecution of Muhammad Abdul Hamid Khalil Salah and Abdelhaleem Hasan Abdelraziq for helping to provide funds to Hamas, the judge denied a government request for an anonymous jury, observing that the defendants were not in custody and that they had strictly adhered to the terms of their release and otherwise posed no danger.

Toledo

In a prosecution of Americans for conspiracy to fight against U.S. forces in Iraq, the judge used an anonymous jury. To minimize prejudice, the judge told the jurors that this was customary in a criminal case.

Sears Tower

For the prosecution of the "Liberty City Seven" for conspiracy to topple the Sears Tower and attack other buildings in various cities, the judge initially did not use an anonymous jury. Because an attorney working for one of the defendants gave a list of the jurors' names to members of a defendant's family, the judge used anonymous juries for the next two trials, which were required because of hung juries.

Fort Dix

In a high-profile trial for conspiracy to attack Fort Dix, the judge used an anonymous jury. Each juror met at one of two secret locations; deputy marshals shuttled the jurors to the courthouse. After the trial, jurors were given contact information for members of the news media, and they could contact them if they wished, but the media were not permitted to initiate the contacts.

Jury Questionnaire

In high-profile or sensitive cases, judges often accommodate the need to ask lots of voir dire questions by using a jury questionnaire. Such a questionnaire should be reviewed carefully to ensure that the questions are clear. Usually, shorter questionnaires are more likely to elicit more complete and thoughtful answers.

Some judges are disinclined to use jury questionnaires, preferring to conduct all voir dire orally, often with carefully prepared questions.

A jury questionnaire is always followed by individual oral voir dire of prospective jurors who have not been excluded on the basis of their questionnaire answers.

The Federal Judicial Center has assembled a selection of jury questionnaires used in national security cases: *National Security Prosecutions: Jury Questionnaires and Preliminary Remarks to Prospective Jurors.*

CASE NOTES

First World Trade Center Bombing

The district judge did not use a jury questionnaire, because "[t]here has been . . . absolutely no showing that jury questionnaires are of any particular help in the selection of a jury in highly publicized cases where a searching voir dire is conducted." *United States v. Salameh*, No. 1:93-cr-180, 1993 WL 364486, at *2 (S.D.N.Y. Sept. 15, 1993).

Plot to Bomb New York City Tunnels and Landmarks

The district judge used a jury questionnaire, which he had seldom done before, and he found it very helpful.

First Prosecution for 1998 Embassy Bombings

In the original trial for the 1998 bombings of American embassies in Kenya and Tanzania, the district judge used a jury questionnaire. The judge discovered that the questionnaire caused many jurors to assume that the court would tell them what penalty would go with each crime, and the questionnaire did not make clear that ultimate decisions on the death penalty would be made by the jury.

Prosecution of a Guantánamo Bay Detainee for 1998 Embassy Bombings

For the 2010 trial of Ahmed Khalfan Ghailani, a onetime fugitive, the district judge used a jury questionnaire. The judge made a special effort to ensure that using the questionnaire would not deprive the court of the benefits of oral voir dire.

Toledo

In a prosecution of Americans for conspiracy to fight against U.S. forces in Iraq, the judge used a jury questionnaire. Had he to do it over again, the judge would have given closer scrutiny to the questionnaire, which was prepared by the attorneys, because some of the questions proved to be confusing to the potential jurors.

Atlanta

For a trial on preparing for violent jihad by, among other things, making casing videos of strategic landmarks, the judge used a jury questionnaire. Prospective jurors filled out the questionnaire a week in advance of voir dire. This gave the lawyers and the court ample time to review the questionnaires to focus follow-up voir dire on the most important issues. The judge bifurcated the questionnaire so that prospective jurors filled out the first part, which focused on general background issues and matters that might affect a panel member's service, before they filled out the second part, which focused on issues related to the nature of the trial, beliefs about Islam, and other case-specific matters.

Sears Tower

For the prosecution of the "Liberty City Seven" for conspiracy to topple the Sears Tower and attack other buildings in various cities, the judge did not use a jury questionnaire. The judge has never used one. She prefers face-to-face voir dire in three phases: first are questions directed to the whole panel, second are individual general qualification questions, and third are more sensitive case-specific individual questions.

Fort Dix

In a high-profile trial for conspiracy to attack Fort Dix, the judge used a jury questionnaire. For five days, approximately 150 prospective jurors reported to the courthouse each day to fill out the questionnaire in the jury room, where the judge greeted them. In the courtroom, the judge and the attorneys reviewed answered questionnaires. Approximately two-thirds of the prospective jurors were disqualified on the basis of the questionnaires alone.

Other Cases

Judges used jury questionnaires in the following cases as well:
- *Detroit*
- *Twentieth Hijacker*
- *Dirty Bomber*
- *Prosecution of a Charity*

Sequestration

If there is a substantial risk to jurors of danger or harassment arising from their service, then judges often arrange for the jurors to report to a secret remote location for transportation to the court by deputy marshals. This is sometimes referred to as partial sequestration, semi-sequestration, or soft sequestration. Full sequestration—secure overnight hotel accommodations for jurors—is sometimes used during the deliberation phase but seldom used before that.

Courts often provide semi-sequestered jurors with extra comforts, such as meals, refreshments, or even games and magazines to use during breaks. Sometimes courts require semi-sequestered jurors to eat lunch together and away from the public.

Judges are cautious about imposing any form of sequestration unnecessarily because of its additional expense, its possible prejudicial impact, and its inconvenience for the jurors.

CASE NOTES

First World Trade Center Bombing

Jurors reported to secret locations from which deputy marshals transported them to court, but jurors were not sequestered overnight. The judge sought to provide the jurors with extra comforts, such as meals and beverages.

Plot to Bomb New York City Tunnels and Landmarks

Jurors reported to secret locations from which deputy marshals transported them to court. Jurors were not sequestered overnight until it was time to deliberate, at which time the judge moved from a schedule of four days a week to seven days a week. The judge sought to provide the jurors with extra comforts, such as meals and beverages.

Prosecution of a Guantánamo Bay Detainee for 1998 Embassy Bombings

In preparation for the 2010 trial of Ahmed Khalfan Ghailani, a onetime fugitive, deputy marshals shuttled the jurors to and from the courthouse and provided them with breakfast, lunch, and refreshments.

Detroit

In the first post-September 11, 2001, prosecution for terrorism, the jurors assembled each morning at a secret location, and they were driven by van to the courthouse. Someone found out about the secret location and called the jury room with a death threat. The marshal changed the jurors' meeting location, used a different-color van to transport them, and beefed up security for the courtroom.

Dirty Bomber

In the Miami trial of three men—including Jose Padilla, who was originally detained as a dirty bomber but ultimately was tried for terrorism conspiracy—potential jurors were shielded from the public during jury selection by a screen in the courthouse lobby.

The jury was semi-sequestered. Jurors did not report directly to the courthouse; they reported to one of two specific secret locations—one on the north side of town and one on the south side—from which they were shuttled to the courthouse. Instead of going their own way for lunch, they always ate together. Once a week or so, the deputy marshals took them out for lunch. Restrooms on the courtroom's floor were reserved for use by jurors and court staff only. Cubicle walls were used to screen off a rest area outside the jury room, a table and chairs were set up outside on a porch, and extra games and magazines were brought in.

Prosecution of a Charity

The prosecution of the Holy Land Foundation and its principals for providing funds to Hamas required two trials because of a hung jury after the first one. The judge presiding over the first trial had jurors meet in a secret location, and even the judge did not know where that was. They were shuttled to the courthouse, and they came to the courtroom floor in a secure elevator. They took lunch in the jury room. The judge presiding over the second trial chose not to use these special procedures so as not to communicate to the jurors that the case was unusual.

Toledo

In a prosecution of Americans for conspiracy to fight against U.S. forces in Iraq, jurors reported to an off-site location instead of to the courthouse. To minimize the prejudicial impact of this procedure, the judge told the jurors that meeting off-site was necessary because of insufficient courthouse parking, which to some extent was actually true.

Sears Tower

The prosecution of the "Liberty City Seven" for conspiracy to topple the Sears Tower and attack other buildings in various cities required three trials because of hung juries. In the first trial, an attorney working for one of the defendants gave a list of the jurors' names to members of a defendant's family, so the judge used an anonymous jury with partial sequestration in the second trial. Jurors met at undisclosed locations and were shuttled to the courthouse; the court provided them with lunch. For the third trial, however, the judge did not use sequestration, because it is a burden on the jurors and an additional operating expense. The judge monitored the situation, however, to see if sequestration would be warranted after all.

Fort Dix

In a high-profile trial for conspiracy to attack Fort Dix, the judge sequestered the jurors at a nearby hotel during deliberations.

Other Cases

Judges semi-sequestered jurors in the following cases as well:
- *First Prosecution for 1998 Embassy Bombings*
- *Millennium Bomber*

News of National Security Events

It will sometimes happen that during a trial related to a significant national security incident another significant national security incident will occur. It may be unreasonable to expect jurors to shield themselves from news of the second event, but judges are likely to caution them not to allow this news to prejudice the participation in the current trial.

CASE NOTES

Plot to Bomb New York City Tunnels and Landmarks

While defendants were being tried for a plot to bomb New York City tunnels and landmarks, related to the 1993 bombing of the World Trade Center, a bomb partially destroyed the federal building in Oklahoma City, including the courthouse there. The district judge permitted the New York jurors to consult news of the event, but admonished them not to let it influence them in the trial.

Special Evidence Issues

Witness Security

It is not uncommon in national security cases for the court to be asked to protect the identity of witnesses. Witnesses against the defendant may include informants who would be at risk if their identities were known; they may even be in the witness protection program. Witnesses may also include covert government agents, including foreign agents or security personnel. With respect to foreign government witnesses, protection of their identity may be a condition of the foreign government's permitting them to testify.

Courts have permitted witnesses to testify under pseudonyms. Courts have also permitted witnesses to use special entrances to the courtroom, often those generally used for prisoners. "Light disguise" is sometimes permitted so long as the disguise does not obscure the witness's demeanor or indicia of credibility. Judges sometimes forbid courtroom sketch artists from sketching the witness's likeness.

Courts have sometimes shielded the witness's face or voice altogether. Although the witness may not be shielded from litigants and court personnel, and from the jury if present at the proceeding, the witness may be shielded from the public either by screens or by use of an audiovisual feed to a second courtroom for the public. The witness's image might be omitted from the video display, and the witness's voice might be electronically altered.

Sometimes the testimony of foreign witnesses must be taken remotely by video deposition. This often includes defense representation both in court and at the foreign deposition location.

Judges are careful not to impose unwarranted or excessive protections.

CASE NOTES

First Prosecution for 1998 Embassy Bombings

An informant testified for the government in the trial for the 1998 bombings of American embassies in Kenya and Tanzania. *In re Terrorist Bombings of U.S. Embassies in East Africa*, 552 F.3d 93, 137–39, 141 (2d Cir. 2008); *United States v. Bin Laden*, 397 F. Supp. 2d 465, 474 (S.D.N.Y. 2005). Prior to his testimony, he was identified, even to defense counsel, only as CS-1, which stood for "confidential source one." In 1996, he separated from Al-Qaeda after embezzling money from one of Osama bin Laden's companies. At an American embassy in Africa, he offered to help fight Al-Qaeda. The U.S. government kept him protected at an undisclosed location after he pleaded guilty in 1997 to a conspiracy charge in a sealed proceeding. *In re Terrorist Bombings*, 552 F.3d at 142; *Bin Laden*, 397 F. Supp. 2d at 474. The informant's identity was not revealed to defense counsel until four days before his scheduled testimony, and a protective order forbade counsel from revealing the informant's identity to the defendants until the day before the informant appeared in court. The district judge forbade courtroom artists from sketching the informant's face.

Prosecution of a Guantánamo Bay Detainee for 1998 Embassy Bombings

In the 2010 trial of onetime fugitive Ahmed Khalfan Ghailani, the judge prohibited a courtroom artist from sketching a witness's face. The witness did not testify at trial, because the judge found that his identity was discovered as a result of extremely harsh interrogation of the defendant. The witness testified at a suppression hearing, however, at a time when the witness's identity was a secret. Because the witness's identity was revealed at the hearing, the judge unredacted his name from court documents.

Millennium Bomber

In the prosecution of Ahmed Ressam, who planned to bomb the Los Angeles International Airport at the turn of the millennium, one of the witnesses against the defendant was Abdelghani Meskini, an accomplice who had pleaded guilty in another jurisdiction. He entered the witness protection program because of his testimony. He used a side door to enter the courtroom.

The district judge overruled the government's attempts to protect the identity of another potential witness, such as by taking testimony remotely or behind a screen and withholding background information, and the government decided not to use the witness.

American Taliban

In the prosecution of John Walker Lindh, who became known as the American Taliban, the defendant pleaded guilty on a day the court was prepared to take testimony from a covert agent on a motion to suppress the defendant's confession. To protect the witness's identity, the district judge worked with the classified information security officers and the U.S. Marshals Service to make adjustments to the courtroom. The courtroom was outfitted with special draperies and screens. The witness box was shielded from the public, as was the path to the door through which prisoners often are brought—a door that would be used in this case for the witness.

The plan was for the defendant and his counsel to sit in the jury box so that they could see the witness, but the draperies shielded the witness from the public's view. *United States v. Rosen*, 520 F. Supp. 2d 786, 795 n.15 (E.D. Va. 2007). The courtroom was equipped with an electronic device that would distort the witness's voice, but the words would be understandable to the parties and the public.

September 11 Damages

In a civil action against alleged supporters of the September 11, 2001, attacks, some plaintiffs introduced as evidence supporting a default judgment against Iran videotaped testimony from Iranian government defectors. To protect the safety of the witnesses and their families, the court allowed the plaintiffs to file both a public brief and a sealed supplemental brief, with the defectors' testimony as sealed exhibits.

Dirty Bomber

In the trial of Jose Padilla, originally detained as a dirty bomber but ultimately tried with two other men for terrorism conspiracy, special security measures were used for a witness who found an incriminating document in Afghanistan. The witness used a special entrance to enter and exit the courtroom, and he reached the floor of the courtroom from the basement in the prisoner elevator. The witness testified under pseudonym and in light disguise: black-rimmed glasses and a closely cropped beard. Sketch artists were prohibited from sketching him, and questioning could not breach CIA personnel and location secrets.

A Plot to Kill President Bush

Ahmed Omar Abu Ali, an American citizen educated at the University of Medina in Saudi Arabia, was convicted of terrorism conspiracy and conspiracy to kill the President. *United States v. Abu Ali*, 528 F.3d 210, 221, 226 (4th Cir. 2008). He was originally arrested in Saudi Arabia by the counterterrorism Mabahith on another matter: an investigation of a 2003 bombing in Riyadh. *Id.* at 223–24, 238; *United States v. Abu Ali*, 395 F. Supp. 2d 338, 341, 344, 367, 384 (E.D. Va. 2005). Mabahith questioning resulted in a confession to facts supporting the American indictment. Because the identities of Mabahith officers are secret, the Saudi government would not permit them to come to the United States to testify. They testified pseudonymously by video deposition conducted in Saudi Arabia. When portions of the depositions were played in court, only the judge, the parties, and the jury could see the video portion, but the public could hear the audio portion.

Prosecution of a Charity

The prosecution of the Holy Land Foundation and its principals for providing funds to Hamas required two trials because of a hung jury after the first one. At both trials, two witnesses testified under cover. Methods of protecting the witnesses' security were established by the judge who presided over the first trial.

Both witnesses testified under pseudonyms, and their identities were not disclosed to defense counsel. One witness was a lawyer in the counterterrorism section of the Israel Security Agency (ISA), also known as Shin Bet, who was to testify as an expert on Hamas financing. Israeli law prohibits the disclosure of ISA agents' identities. The other witness worked for the Israeli Defense Forces, which looks to ISA rules for the protection of its personnel.

The courtroom was closed to the public and the news media during these witnesses' testimony, but the defendants and their immediate family members were permitted to attend. The witnesses entered and exited the courtroom through a non-public door. The public and the news media could listen to an audio feed in another courtroom. In response to any question under cross-examination that called on them to reveal classified information, the witnesses were permitted to consult counsel.

Chicago

In the prosecution of Muhammad Abdul Hamid Khalil Salah for helping to provide funds to Hamas, Salah sought testimony from two Israel Security Agency (ISA) agents to prove that his confession in Israel was obtained by torture and coercion. *United States v. Abu Marzook*, 412 F. Supp. 2d 913, 916 (N.D. Ill. 2006). It was unprecedented for such officers to provide testimony outside of Israel.

The identities of ISA agents are kept secret by Israel. The judge agreed to close the hearing on Salah's motion to suppress his confession while the ISA agents testified. *United States v. Marzook*, 435 F. Supp. 2d 708, 714 (N.D. Ill. 2006); *Abu Marzook*, 412 F. Supp. 2d 913. The government of Israel waived its secret classification of the agents' testimony as to defense attorneys and Salah. All other persons in court during the testimony had security clearances.

To protect the agents' identities, they were permitted to use private entrances to the courthouse and the courtroom. The agents and their Israeli attorneys were identified in court documents by code names. But the judge denied a request that they testify in "light disguise," because Salah had already seen them, the public would not see them, and the government had presented no evidence of security concerns respecting the attorneys and court staff who would see them.

The hearing, which was conducted intermittently over the course of several weeks, was open for the testimony of other witnesses, including Israeli police officers.

For the trial, the judge again permitted the ISA agents to testify using pseudonyms in a closed courtroom. Again the judge permitted the witnesses to use private entrances. She permitted the defendants' immediate family members to remain in the courtroom during the agents' testimony. Because of the presence of the family members and the jury, the judge agreed to let the agents testify in light disguise, so long as the disguises did not interfere with the jurors' ability to judge the witnesses' credibility. But the agents ultimately decided to testify without disguise, because of the limitations on who would be in the courtroom to see them. The judge decided that the rest of the trial would be public.

The closed portion of the trial was kept as open as possible. The court established a live video and audio feed to another courtroom where spectators could listen to the closed session and see those in the courtroom, except for the witnesses. To disguise from the jury that the courtroom was closed, the jurors were told that the camera was a precaution in case of an overflow crowd, and the witnesses used the private entrance before the jury was brought in.

Toledo

A prosecution of Americans for conspiracy to fight against U.S. forces in Iraq was based, in part, on evidence from a government informant, called "the Trainer" in the indictment, who was hired to see who in the Toledo-area Muslim community would respond positively to professed approval of overseas jihad. The identity of the witness was initially a secret, but newspapers revealed his name, so the judge issued an order forbidding public dissemination of his image or identity.

Foreign Evidence

Foreign witnesses are beyond the court's subpoena power. The witnesses may consent to travel to the United States to offer testimony, which may require permission from their government if they are government officers. A condition of this travel may be security measures to protect the witness's identity.

Testimony might also be taken remotely by video deposition. Typically the witness is abroad and the defendant is local and an audiovisual link is established to provide for adequate confrontation. Lawyers for each side are typically at both locations, and a communication link is established so that the defendant can confer with defense counsel at both locations. The judge might be either at the home court or at the foreign location.

CASE NOTES

Millennium Bomber

In the prosecution of Ahmed Ressam, who planned to bomb the Los Angeles International Airport at the turn of the millennium, the government sought testimony of witnesses in Canada, beyond the court's subpoena power, who were unwilling to travel to the United States to offer testimony. By stipulation of the parties, the judge traveled to Canada to preside over video depositions in both Montreal and Vancouver to obtain the testimony. A Canadian court official attended to rule on potential issues of Canadian law. Ressam participated by videoconference from his jail cell with the assistance of an Arabic interpreter.

On one occasion, after the American judge had traveled to Canada for the deposition, a Canadian judge ruled, at a proceeding from which the American judge was excluded, that the witness did not have to testify.

Some of the witnesses subsequently indicated that they might be willing to testify live at Ressam's trial, but the parties agreed that either side could substitute deposition videotapes.

The federal defender's office represented Ressam, and the office agreed to accept service on his behalf of three seizure notices from the Royal Canadian Mounted Police. Two attorneys and an investigator traveled to Montreal to investigate the seizures, and they obtained from the Canadian court copies of documents in the related files. Apparently, the documents were disclosed to the attorneys in error and were taken back at the Montreal airport. The U.S. prosecution moved for an order prohibiting the attorneys from discussing the documents with their client. The district judge told the attorneys that they could only use the information they obtained from the Canadian files as a last resort, and they could not disclose to their client the origin of the information.

Guantánamo Bay

Guantánamo Bay detainees who wished to testify at their habeas hearings had to do so by secure video link, because the government was unwilling to transport them to court. A habeas attorney and an interpreter, if necessary, were in Guantánamo Bay. Another habeas attorney was in the courtroom with the judge and the government's attorney, possibly with additional interpreters.

A Plot to Kill President Bush

Ahmed Omar Abu Ali, an American citizen convicted of terrorism conspiracy and conspiracy to kill the President, was originally arrested in Saudi Arabia by the counterterrorism Mabahith in an investigation of a 2003 bombing in Riyadh. *United States v. Abu Ali*, 528 F.3d 210, 221, 223–24, 226, 238 (4th Cir. 2008); *United States v. Abu Ali*, 395 F. Supp. 2d 338, 341, 344, 367, 384 (E.D. Va. 2005). Because the identities of Mabahith officers are secret, the Saudi government would not permit them to come to the United States to testify. Instead, they testified pseudonymously by video deposition conducted in Saudi Arabia. The district judge sent to Saudi Arabia two prosecutors, two defense attorneys, a camera operator, and an interpreter. (If the judge had it to do over again, he would have sent at least one relief interpreter.) A live video feed was established between Saudi Arabia and the U.S. courtroom, in which were the judge, additional counsel for both sides, and the court reporter. The video image was constructed as a split screen with the defendant on one side and the witness on the other, so that the defendant could see the witness and the witness could see the defendant. The defendant could communicate with his attorneys in Saudi Arabia via cell phone during breaks or on request.

Challenges posed by this remote video deposition included the time-zone difference, the unreliable availability of a secure connection, and Saudi Arabian heat that sometimes caused technical difficulties.

Prosecution of a Charity

In the prosecution of the Holy Land Foundation and its principals for providing funds to Hamas, two Israeli witnesses testified under cover: one witness was a lawyer in the counterterrorism section of Shin Bet, the Israel Security Agency; the other witness worked for the Israeli Defense Forces.

Chicago

In the prosecution of Muhammad Abdul Hamid Khalil Salah for helping to provide funds to Hamas, Salah sought testimony from two Israel Security Agency (ISA) agents to prove that his confession in Israel was obtained by torture and coercion. *United States v. Abu Marzook*, 412 F. Supp. 2d 913, 916 (N.D. Ill. 2006). It was unprecedented for such officers to provide testimony outside of Israel. Israel permitted the witnesses to travel to the United States to provide testimony, and the court applied security measures to protect the secrecy of their identities.

Salah also sought to discover Israeli police documents to support his claim that his confession while in custody in Israel was obtained by torture and coercion. The judge suggested that he follow rogatory-letter procedures, but Salah ultimately relied on testimony from Israeli police officers.

Examination of High-Security Detainees

Sometimes national security defendants seek testimony from persons who are in custody for national security reasons. The government is frequently reluctant to permit examination of such detainees, but some examination may be necessary to afford the defendant an adequate defense. Solutions to these competing interests have sometimes involved not direct examination but examination through interrogators.

CASE NOTES

American Taliban

In the prosecution of John Walker Lindh, who became known as the American Taliban, defense counsel wanted to interview persons detained at Guantánamo Bay. The district judge denied face-to-face access to the detainees, but the judge established a procedure allowing counsel to submit questions to "firewall" government attorneys who passed them on to the detainees.

Firewall attorneys included attorneys from the Department of Justice and the Department of Defense "who are separate and independent from the attorneys who represent the government" in the case, including two assistant U.S. attorneys from another district.

Defense counsel submitted questions for each detainee to the firewall attorneys. The firewall attorneys could object to any questions, and the court would resolve any objections on sealed noticed filings. Approved questions were submitted to interrogators who interwove the questions into the interrogations. Firewall attorneys prepared written summaries, and defense counsel could submit follow-up questions. Soon thereafter, the firewall attorneys submitted to defense counsel video recordings of the interviews.

The judge monitored the procedure to ensure that it protected Lindh's rights to a defense.

Senior Government Officers

In national security cases, attorneys sometimes seek evidence from national security policy makers. Judges are cautious about allowing these cases to interfere with the important work of senior government officers. Judges will allow such interference, however, if justice so requires.

CASE NOTES

First Prosecution for 1998 Embassy Bombings

In the prosecution for the 1998 bombing of American embassies in Kenya and Tanzania, Mohamed Rashed Daoud al-'Owhali's attorneys decided that testimony from Secretary of State Madeleine Albright about the impact of U.S. sanctions on Iraqi citizens might be helpful during the penalty phase of the trial. The district judge initially agreed to sign the subpoena, but on the government's motion he quashed it. Al-'Owhali presented at trial as a substitute for her live testimony a *60 Minutes* interview with Secretary Albright. Al-'Owhali also presented similar evidence through a willing witness, former Attorney General Ramsey Clark.

Detroit

In the first post-September 11, 2001, prosecution for terrorism, the judge issued "a public and formal judicial admonishment of the Attorney General." *United States v. Koubriti*, 305 F. Supp. 2d 723, 726 (E.D. Mich. 2003); *see id.* at 763–65. Eight days after the judge issued a stipulated gag order forbidding public comments about the case that would have a reasonable likelihood of interfering with a fair trial, the Attorney General incorrectly stated at a press conference that the defendants were "suspected of having knowledge of the September 11th attacks." *Id.* at 725, 728–30, 733. Also, during the trial, the Attorney General commented favorably at a press conference on the credibility of a cooperating codefendant's testimony. The stipulated admonishment avoided the Attorney General's having to testify at a contempt hearing.

Guantánamo Bay

To resolve a motion to enjoin a Guantánamo Bay detainee's transfer to Algeria, where he feared he would be tortured or killed, the district court ordered testimony from the special envoy for the closure of the Guantánamo Bay detention facility, who had the rank of ambassador, because the court determined that the ambassador's declaration opposing the motion lacked specificity. The government refused to provide the testimony, the district court enjoined the transfer, and the court of appeals dissolved the injunction.

Giving State Secrets to Lobbyists

In a sting prosecution of lobbyists for sharing classified information, the defendants requested subpoenas for 20 current and former high-ranking government officials, including Secretary of State Condolezza Rice, because of her former position as National Security Advisor. *United States v. Rosen*, 520 F. Supp. 2d 802, 804, 806–07 (E.D. Va. 2007). The judge sustained the government's objection as to five witnesses, but overruled its objection as to the following: Secretary Rice; current National Security Advisor Stephen Hadley, who was her deputy; Paul Wolfowitz and Richard Armitage, each formerly Deputy Secretary of State; and seven others. Recognizing that the requested testimony would be more credible and probative than alternatives, the judge observed that "nothing in the Sixth Amendment right to compulsory process requires, nor should it require, an accused to refrain from calling government officials as witnesses until he has exhausted possible nongovernmental witnesses to prove a fact." *Id.* at 811.

Pro Se Issues

A defendant's exercising his or her right to pro se representation is usually a substantial complication.

The first line of defense against this complication is prevention. Judges will sometimes remedy bad fits between appointed counsel and defendants.

A defendant in a national security case may wish to use court proceedings to make a public statement. Judges often set limits with defendants so that they do not have both all the benefits of appointed counsel and opportunities to use court proceedings for personal proclamations. Such limits are usually set delicately. For example, a defendant who wishes to personally make an opening statement may be required to proceed through the trial pro se as a consequence.

Courts frequently appoint standby counsel for pro se defendants, even against the defendants' wishes. Courts may withdraw the pro se privilege if it is abused or if the defendant's exercise of the privilege becomes too disruptive.

If classified information is at issue in the case, the court may have to appoint counsel to handle classified issues, because the government may choose not to give the defendant access to classified information.

CASE NOTES

First World Trade Center Bombing

The four defendants convicted in 1994 of bombing the World Trade Center in 1993 dismissed their attorneys after they were convicted by the jury. *United States v. Salameh*, 856 F. Supp. 781, 782 (S.D.N.Y. 1994). They appeared at sentencing pro se. *United States v. Salameh*, 152 F.3d 88, 161 (1998). In 1998, the court of appeals vacated their sentences because the record did not reflect a knowing, intelligent, and voluntary waiver of their rights to counsel. In 1999, the defendants were resentenced, and those sentences were affirmed in 2001. *United States v. Salameh*, 261 F.3d 271 (2d Cir. 2001).

Plot to Bomb U.S. Airplanes in Southeast Asia

Ramzi Ahmed Yousef was a defendant in the prosecution for the 1993 bombing of the World Trade Center, but at the time of the 1993–1994 trial, Yousef was a fugitive. *Salameh*, 152 F.3d at 108. In 1995, because of an accidental home fire, he was discovered mixing bomb chemicals in Manila, Philippines, and this discovery led to a prosecution for a plot to blow up American air carriers' planes in southeast Asian routes. *United States v. Yousef*, 327 F.3d 56, 79–81 (2d Cir. 2003). Yousef initially eluded arrest, but he was apprehended the following month in Islamabad, Pakistan. At his trial for the Asian bomb plot, he asked to address the jury during opening arguments. The district judge said that if he did that, he would have to represent himself throughout the trial, and Yousef agreed to do that. He was convicted. At his later trial for the World Trade Center bombing, he allowed a lawyer to represent him. He was convicted again.

Twentieth Hijacker

At a hearing on conditions of confinement, four months after his indictment, Zacarias Moussaoui announced that he would like to represent himself, possibly with the assistance of a Muslim attorney, because his assigned attorneys did not understand Muslims. *United States v. Moussaoui*, 591 F.3d 263, 269–70 (4th Cir. 2010); *United States v. Moussaoui*, 333 F.3d 509, 512–13 (4th Cir. 2003).

A court-appointed psychiatrist determined that Moussaoui was a fanatic, but not mentally incompetent to stand trial or waive his right to counsel. The judge granted Moussaoui's motion to represent himself, keeping appointed counsel as standbys.

Nineteen months later, the judge revoked Moussaoui's right to proceed pro se, because of frequent inappropriate filings.

Once he began to proceed pro se, Moussaoui began to file with the court handwritten documents that the court regarded as motions. The district judge observed, "The defendant's pleadings have been replete with irrelevant, inflammatory and insulting rhetoric, which would not be tolerated from an attorney practicing in this court." Pro Se Filings Sealing Order at 3, *United States v. Moussaoui*, No. 1:01-cr-455 (E.D. Va. Aug. 29, 2002), available at 2002 WL 1990900. The government also became concerned that the filings might include coded messages to confederates. One remedy was to seal Moussaoui's filings, but the news media were vigilant in advocating for a minimum of sealing. In general, the filings were initially sealed and then unsealed or redacted after a review by the government and the court.

Atlanta

Two young men were prosecuted in Atlanta for preparing for violent jihad by, among other things, making casing videos of strategic landmarks. As trial approached, each of the defendants expressed an interest in representing himself. The government decided to try the two defendants separately. Syed Haris Ahmed opted for a bench trial, but accepted representation by counsel. Ehsanul Islam Sadequee announced on the first day of jury selection that he would represent himself. The judge appointed his attorneys as standby counsel. Sadequee cross-examined the government's witnesses but did not call any witnesses himself. For his defense, he offered only his own testimony and closing argument. Both defendants were convicted.

The Federal Judicial Center

Board

The Chief Justice of the United States, *Chair*
Judge Susan H. Black, U.S. Court of Appeals for the Eleventh Circuit
Magistrate Judge John Michael Facciola, U.S. District Court for the District of Columbia
Judge James B. Haines, Jr., U.S. Bankruptcy Court for the District Maine
Judge James F. Holderman, Jr., U.S. District Court for the Northern District of Illinois
Judge Edward C. Prado, U.S. Court of Appeals for the Fifth Circuit
Judge Loretta A. Preska, U.S. District Court for the Southern District of New York
Judge Kathryn H. Vratil, U.S. District Court for the District of Kansas
Judge Thomas F. Hogan, Director of the Administrative Office of the U.S. Courts

Director
Judge Jeremy D. Fogel

Deputy Director
John S. Cooke

About the Federal Judicial Center

The Federal Judicial Center is the research and education agency of the federal judicial system. It was established by Congress in 1967 (28 U.S.C. §§ 620–629), on the recommendation of the Judicial Conference of the United States.

By statute, the Chief Justice of the United States chairs the Center's Board, which also includes the director of the Administrative Office of the U.S. Courts and seven judges elected by the Judicial Conference.

The organization of the Center reflects its primary statutory mandates. The Education Division plans and produces education and training programs for judges and court staff, including satellite broadcasts, video programs, publications, curriculum packages for in-court training, and Web-based programs and resources. The Research Division examines and evaluates current and alternative federal court practices and policies. This research assists Judicial Conference committees, who request most Center research, in developing policy recommendations. The Center's research also contributes substantially to its educational programs. The two divisions work closely with two units of the Director's Office—the Systems Innovation & Development Office and Communications Policy & Design Office—in using print, broadcast, and online media to deliver education and training and to disseminate the results of Center research. The Federal Judicial History Office helps courts and others study and preserve federal judicial history. The International Judicial Relations Office provides information to judicial and legal officials from foreign countries and assesses how to inform federal judicial personnel of developments in international law and other court systems that may affect their work.

www.ingramcontent.com/pod-product-compliance
Lightning Source LLC
Chambersburg PA
CBHW081254180526
45170CB00007B/2422